Doggin'

The 100 Best Places To Hike With Your Dog In The Free State

DOUG GELBERT

illustrations by

ANDREW CHESWORTH

Cruden Bay Books

There is always a new trail to look forward to...

DOGGIN' MARYLAND: THE 100 BEST PLACES TO HIKE
WITH YOUR DOG IN THE FREE STATE

Copyright 2006 by Cruden Bay Books

Cruden Bay Books
PO Box 467
Montchanin, DE 19710
www.hikewithyourdog.com

International Standard Book Number 978-09795577-4-3

*"Dogs are our link to paradise...to sit with a dog on a hillside
on a glorious afternoon is to be back in Eden,
where doing nothing was not boring - it was peace."*
- Milan Kundera

Ahead On The Trail

Introduction

Maryland can be a great place to hike with your dog. Within an couple hours' drive from most anywhere in the state you can hike on sand trails, climb mountains that leave your dog panting, walk on some of the most historic grounds in America, explore the estates of America's wealthiest families or circle lakes for miles and never lose sight of the water.

I have selected what I consider to be the 100 best places to take your dog for an outing and ranked them according to subjective criteria including the variety of hikes available, opportunities for canine swimming and pleasure of the walks. The rankings include a mix of parks that feature long walks and parks that contain short walks. Did I miss your favorite? Let us know at *www.hikewithyourdog.com*.

For dog owners it is important to realize that not all parks are open to our best trail companions (see page 14 for a list of parks that do not allow dogs). It is sometimes hard to believe but not everyone loves dogs. We are, in fact, in the minority when compared with our non-dog owning neighbors.

So when visiting a park always keep your dog under control and clean up any messes and we can all expect our great parks to remain open to our dogs. And maybe some others will see the light as well. Remember, every time you go out with your dog you are an ambassador for all dog owners.

Grab that leash and hit the trail!
DBG

Hiking With Your Dog

So you want to start hiking with your dog. Hiking with your dog can be a fascinating way to explore Maryland from a canine perspective. Some things to consider:

·🐾· Dog's Health

Hiking can be a wonderful preventative for any number of physical and behavioral disorders. One in every three dogs is overweight and running up trails and leaping through streams is great exercise to help keep pounds off. Hiking can also relieve boredom in a dog's routine and calm dogs prone to destructive habits. And hiking with your dog strengthens the overall owner/dog bond.

·🐾· Breed of Dog

All dogs enjoy the new scents and sights of a trail. But some dogs are better suited to hiking than others. If you don't as yet have a hiking companion, select a breed that matches your interests. Do you look forward to an entire afternoon's hiking? You'll need a dog bred to keep up with such a pace, such as a retriever or a spaniel. Is a half-hour enough walking for you? It may not be for an energetic dog like a border collie. If you already have a hiking friend, tailor your plans to his abilities.

·🐾· Conditioning

Just like humans, dogs need to be acclimated to the task at hand. An inactive dog cannot be expected to bounce from the easy chair in the den to complete a 3-hour hike. You must also be physically able to restrain your dog if confronted with distractions on the trail (like a scampering squirrel or a pack of joggers). Have your dog checked by a veterinarian before significantly increasing his activity level.

·🐾· Weather

Hot humid summers do not do dogs any favors. With no sweat glands and only panting available to disperse body heat, dogs are much more susceptible to heat stroke than we are. Unusually rapid panting and/or a bright red tongue are signs of heat exhaustion in your pet.

Always carry enough water for your hike. Even days that don't seem too warm can cause discomfort in dark-coated dogs if the sun is shining brightly. In cold weather, short-coated breeds may require additional attention.

🐾 Trail Hazards

Dogs won't get poison ivy but they can transfer it to you. Stinging nettle is a nuisance plant that lurks on the side of many trails and the slightest brush will deliver troublesome needles into a dog's coat. Some trails are littered with small pieces of broken glass that can slice a dog's paws. Nasty thorns can also blanket trails that we in shoes may never notice.

🐾 Ticks

You won't be able to spend much time in Maryland parks without encountering ticks. All are nasty but the deer tick - no bigger than a pin head - carries with it the spectre of Lyme disease. Lyme disease attacks a dog's joints and makes walking painful. The tick needs to be embedded in the skin to transmit Lyme disease. It takes 4-6 hours for a tick to become embedded and another 24-48 hours to transmit Lyme disease bacteria.

When hiking, walk in the middle of trails away from tall grass and bushes. And when the summer sun fades away don't stop thinking about ticks - they remain active any time the temperature is above 30 degrees. By checking your dog - and yourself - thoroughly after each walk you can help avoid Lyme disease. Ticks tend to congregate on your dog's ears, between the toes and around the neck and head.

🐾 Water

Surface water, including fast-flowing streams, is likely to be infested with a microscopic protozoa called *Giardia*, waiting to wreak havoc on a dog's intestinal system. The most common symptom is crippling diarrhea. Algae, pollutants and contaminants can all be in streams, ponds and puddles. If possible, carry fresh water for your dog on the trail - your dog can even learn to drink happily from a squirt bottle.

Rattlesnakes

Rattlesnakes are not particularly aggressive animals but you should treat any venomous snake with respect and keep your distance. A rattler's colors may vary but they are recognized by the namesake rattle on the tail and a diamond-shaped head. Unless cornered or teased by humans or dogs, a rattlesnake will crawl away and avoid striking. Avoid placing your hand in unexamined rocky areas and crevasses and try and keep your dog from doing so as well. If you hear a nearby rattle, stop immediately and hold your dog back. Identify where the snake is and slowly back away.

If you or your dog is bitten, do not panic but get to a hospital or veterinarian with as little physical movement as possible. Wrap between the bite and the heart. Rattlesnakes might give "dry bites" where no poison is injected, but you should always check with a doctor after a bite even if you feel fine.

Black Bears

Are you likely to see a bear while out hiking with your dog? No, it's not likely. it is, however, quite a thrill if you are fortunate enough to spot a black bear on the trail - from a distance.

Black bear attacks are incredibly rare. In the year 2000 a hiker was killed by a black bear in Great Smoky National Park and it was the first deadly bear attack in the 66-year history of America's most popular national park. It was the first EVER in the southeastern United States. In all of North America only 43 black bear mauling deaths have ever been recorded (through 1999).

Most problems with black bears occur near a campground (like the above incident) where bears have learned to forage for unprotected food. On the trail bears will typically see you and leave the area. What should you do if you encounter a black bear? Experts agree on three important things:

1) Never run. A bear will outrun you, outclimb you, outswim you. Don't look like prey.
2) Never get between a female bear and a cub who may be nearby feeding.
3) Leave a bear an escape route.

If the bear is at least 15 feet away and notices you make sure you keep your dog close and calm. If a bear stands on its hind legs or comes closer it may just be trying to get a better view or smell to evaluate the situation. Wave your arms and make noise to scare the bear away. Most bears will quickly leave the area.

If you encounter a black bear at close range, stand upright and make yourself appear as large a foe as possible. Avoid direct eye contact and speak in a calm, assertive and assuring voice as you back up slowly and out of danger.

Porcupines

Porcupines are easy for a curious dog to catch and that makes them among the most dangerous animals you may meet because an embedded quill is not only painful but can cause infection if not properly removed.

Outfitting Your Dog For A Hike

These are the basics for taking your dog on a hike:

▸ **Collar.**
It should not be so loose as to come off but you should be able to slide your flat hand under the collar.

▸ **Identification Tags.**
Get one with your veterinarian's phone number as well.

▸ **Bandanna.**
Can help distinguish him from game in hunting season.

▸ **Leash.**
Leather lasts forever but if there's water in your dog"s future, consider quick-drying nylon.

▸ **Water.**
Carry 8 ounces for every hour of hiking.

🐾 *I want my dog to help carry water, snacks and other supplies on the trail. Where do I start?*

To select an appropriate dog pack measure your dog's girth around the rib cage. A dog pack should fit securely without hindering the dog's ability to walk normally.

🐾 *Will my dog wear a pack?*

Wearing a dog pack is no more obtrusive than wearing a collar, although some dogs will take to a pack easier than others. Introduce the pack by draping a towel over your dog's back in the house and then having your dog wear an empty pack on short walks. Progressively add some crumpled newspaper and then bits of clothing. Fill the pack with treats and reward your dog from the stash. Soon your dog will associate the dog pack with an outdoor adventure and will eagerly look forward to wearing it.

🐾 *How much weight can I put into a dog pack?*

Many dog packs are sold by weight recommendations. A healthy, well-conditioned dog can comfortably carry 25% to 33% of its body weight. Breeds prone to back problems or hip dysplasia should not wear dog packs. Consult your veterinarian before stuffing the pouches with gear.

🐾 *How does a dog wear a pack?*

The pack, typically with cargo pouches on either side, should ride as close to the shoulders as possible without limiting movement. The straps that hold the dog pack in place should be situated where they will not cause chafing.

🐾 *What are good things to put in a dog pack?*

Low density items such as food and poop bags are good choices. Ice cold bottles of water can cool your dog down on hot days. Don't put anything in a dog pack that can break. Dogs will bang the pack on rocks and trees as they wiggle through tight spots in the trail. Dogs also like to lie down in creeks and other wet spots so seal items in plastic bags. A good use for dog packs when on day hikes around Maryland is trail maintenance - your dog can pack out trash left by inconsiderate visitors before you.

🐾 *Are dog booties a good idea?*

Dog booties can be an asset, especially for the occasional canine hiker whose paw pads have not become toughened. Some trails around Maryland involve rocky terrain. In some places, there may be broken glass. Hiking boots for dogs are designed to prevent pads from cracking while trotting across rough surfaces. Used in winter, dog booties provide warmth and keep ice balls from forming between toe pads when hiking through snow.

🐾 *What should a doggie first aid kit include?*

Even when taking short hikes it is a good idea to have some basics available for emergencies:

- 4" square gauze pads
- cling type bandaging tapes
- topical wound disinfectant cream
- tweezers
- insect repellent - no reason to leave your dog unprotected against mosquitoes and blackflies
- veterinarian's phone number

*"I can't think of anything that brings me closer to tears than
when my old dog - completely exhausted after a hard day
in the field - limps away from her nice spot in front of the fire
and comes over to where I'm sitting and puts her head in my lap,
a paw over my knee, and closes her eyes, and goes back to sleep.
I don't know what I've done to deserve that kind of friend."*
-Gene Hill

Low Impact Hiking
With Your Dog

Every time you hike with your dog on the trail you are an ambassador for all dog owners. Some people you meet won't believe in your right to take a dog on the trail. Be friendly to all and make the best impression you can by practicing low impact hiking with your dog:

- Pack out everything you pack in.

- Do not leave dog scat on the trail; if you haven't brought plastic bags for poop removal bury it away from the trail and topical water sources.

- Hike only where dogs are allowed.

- Stay on the trail.

- Do not allow your dog to chase wildlife.

- Step off the trail and wait with your dog while horses and other hikers pass.

- Do not allow your dog to bark - people are enjoying the trail for serenity.

- *Have as much fun on your hike as your dog does.*

The Other End Of The Leash

Leash laws are like speed limits - everyone seems to have a private interpretation of their validity. Some dog owners never go outside with an unleashed dog; others treat the laws as suggestions or disregard them completely. It is not the purpose of this book to tell dog owners where to go to evade the leash laws or reveal the parks where rangers will look the other way at an unleashed dog. Nor is it the business of this book to preach vigilant adherence to the leash laws. Nothing written in a book is going to change people's behavior with regard to leash laws. So this will be the last time leash laws are mentioned, save occasionally when we point out the parks where dogs are welcomed off leash.

How To Pet A Dog
Tickling tummies slowly and gently works wonders.
Never use a rubbing motion; this makes dogs bad-tempered.
A gentle tickle with the tips of the fingers is all that is necessary
to induce calm in a dog. I hate strangers who go up to dogs with their
hands held to the dog's nose, usually palm towards themselves.
How does the dog know that the hand doesn't hold something horrid?
The palm should always be shown to the dog and go straight
down to between the dog's front legs and tickle gently with
a soothing voice to accompany the action.
Very often the dog raises its back leg in a scratching movement,
it gets so much pleasure from this.
-Barbara Woodhouse

No Dogs

Before we get started on the best places to take your dog, let's get out of the way some of the trails that do not allow dogs:

Allegany County
Dan's Mountain State Park

Anne Arundel County
Jug Bay Wetlands Sanctuary
Sandy Point State Park

Baltimore County
Hart-Miller Island State Park
(dogs are allowed on Pleasure Island, accessible only by boat and with no formal trails)
Patapsco State Park - Avalon Area, Hollofield Area, McKeldin Area, Orange Grove Area

Calvert County
Breezy Point Beach
Calvert Cliffs State Park

Caroline County
Martinak State Park

Charles County
Myrtle Grove Wildlife Management Area
Smallwood State Park

Dorchester County
Blackwater National Wildlife Refuge

Frederick County
Cunningham Falls State Park

Garrett County
Deep Creek Lake State Park
Herrington Manor State Park
New Germany State Park

Montgomery County
Seneca Creek State Park - Clopper Day Use Area

Queen Anne's County
Chesapeake Bay Environmental Center

Washington County
Fort Frederick State Park
Greenbrier State Park
Hagerstown City Park
Washington Monument State Park

Worcester County
Assateague State Park
Pocomoke River State Park - Shad Landing

O.K. that wasn't too bad. Let's forget about these and move on to some of the great places where we CAN take our dogs across Maryland...

The Best of the Best

1. Catoctin Mountain Park
What are you looking for on an outing with your dog - a variety of short, peaceful hikes? A strenuous , multi-hour trek that will have your dog sleeping the whole ride home? Memorable views? Catoctin has them all. If it's good enough for the Presidential dogs, it should be good enough for our dogs.

2. Tuckahoe State Park
The place to go for a hike with your dog on the Eastern Shore. Your dog won't find any trails that are more paw-friendly than the grassy meadows and sandy dirt of the Adkins Arboretum.

3. Robert E. Lee Park
With its rough-around-the-edges look, Robert E. Lee radiates plenty of canine charm. It feels as if dogs are welcome here and the 456-acre park has evolved into a prime destination for dog walkers of all sorts. Looking for a quick walk and a swim? Lake Roland can't be beat for deep water dog paddling. After a half-day's outing with your dog on the hiking trails? Cross the light rail line and the trail system explodes into a maze of hard-packed dirt passageways through the woods. Just need to let the dog romp with some buddies? Robert E. Lee Park may as well be Rover E. Lee Park. You'll find more dogs per hour here than any park in the Baltimore area.

4. Susquehanna State Park
The first European to set eyes on the Susquehanna River was English explorer John Smith. He was suitably impressed. "Heaven and earth," he wrote, "seemed never to have agreed better to frame a place for man's commodious and delightful habitation." Dog owners might readily concur. At Susquehanna State Park you can test trails in the hills that will leave man and dog panting or stroll along the shady Susquehanna and Tidewater Canal towpath, as level and pleasant an excursion as you can take with your dog.

5. Harpers Ferry National Historic Park
No place in Maryland packs as much scenic wonder and historical importance for your dog into such a small area as Harpers Ferry National Historic Park where the Shenandoah and Potomac rivers join forces.

6. Downs Memorial Park

Looking for a dog-friendly park? At Downs Memorial Park there is a "pet parking" stall outside the information center. A dog drinking bowl is chained to a human water fountain. The walking is fine too. Some five miles of easy hiking through woodlands of oak and maple and holly and gum. Best of all is Dog Beach, an isolated, scruffy 40-yard stretch of sand where you can let the dog off leash for canine aquatics in the Chesapeake Bay. The wave action is just right for dogs and there is enough sand for digging. Need we say more?

7. Sugarloaf Mountain

The quarter-million human visitors aren't the only ones who appreciate this wonderful private gift to the public - dogs love these mountain trails as well.

8. Assateague National Seashore

You can bring your dog here to swim in the ocean in the middle of the summer. Nuff said!

9. Swallow Falls State Park

This is the best single-trail park in Maryland. Even though dogs can't use the trail between Memorial Day and Labor Day it still rates in the Top Ten. It's that good.

10. Gunpowder Falls State Park - Hereford

At Hereford the canine hiker can find any length or type of hike to set tails wagging. Long out-and-back walks through a rugged gorge (this is Baltimore?) can be combined with many side trails that scamper up the valley slopes. You'll find plenty of great canine swimming holes in the river, fed by outflows from the Prettyboy Dam. You can even take the dog right to the base of the dam on a narrow trail drenched in mountain laurel.

*"What counts is not necessarily the size of the dog
in the fight but the size of the fight in the dog."*
-Dwight D. Eisenhower

The 100 Best Places To Hike With Your Dog In Maryland...

1
Catoctin Mountain Park

The Park

It took an offer of 200 acres of land rent free for three years and a penny an acre thereafter by Lord Baltimore to lure settlers into this remote region. When they finally came so much wood was cut for charcoal, tanning and lumber that eventually people left the mountains. This time there was no effort to populate the region and in 1935 over 10,000 acres were acquired by the Federal Government and developed as the Catoctin Recreational Demonstration Area. The land regenerated into an eastern hardwood climax forest looking again as it did before the original European settlement.

> ### Frederick
>
> Phone Number
> - (301) 663-9388
>
> Website
> - www.nps.gov/cato
>
> Admission Fee
> - None
>
> Directions
> - The Visitor Center, where you can pick up many of the park trails, is on MD 77, west of US Route 15 in Thurmont.

Everyone has heard of Camp David but where exactly it is? Surprisingly it is located right here in Catoctin Mountain Park. When you take your dog there, you will never see Camp David or any evidence that the presidential compound is hidden among the trees but the trails you can hike on are of Presidential quality nonetheless.

The Walks

You could fill up a day of canine hiking at Catoctin Mountain Park just by checking off the many easy self-guiding interpretive trails as you learn about mountain culture and forest ecology.

There is plenty of more challenging fare in the park as well. Three of the best vistas - Wolf Rock, Chimney Rock and Cat Rock - are connected by a rollercoaster trail on the eastern edge of the mountain. There is little understory in the woods and views are long. Many of the mountain slope trails are rocky and footing can be uncertain under paw on climbs to 1500 feet.

In the western region of Catoctin Mountain, near the Owens Creek campground, are wide horse trails ideal for contemplative canine hiking.

The forests deep in the rugged Catoctin Mountains provided ideal cover for a whiskey still, made illegal by the onset of Prohibition in 1919. On a steaming July day in 1929 Federal agents raided the Blue Blazes Whiskey Still and confiscated more than 25,000 gallons of mash. Today the airy, wooded *Blue Blazes Whiskey Trail* along Distillery Run leads to a recreated working still and interprets the history of whiskey making in the backwoods of Appalachia.

A short hike on the Blue Blazes Whiskey Trail takes your dog to a reproduction of a working still.

The grades are gentler for long hikes through mixed hardwoods of chestnut oak, hickory, black birch and yellow poplar.

Trail Sense: Excellent maps and trail markings will not leave you stranded.

Dog Friendliness

Dogs are allowed in the campground and on all national park trails but not across the road in the popular Cunningham Falls State Park.

Traffic

Most trails are hiker-only and you can usually find a good stretch of solitude in Catoctin Mountain.

Canine Swimming

Small streams percolate through the mountains but there are no great swimming holes.

Trail Time

A full day is possible.

2
Tuckahoe State Park

The Park

The easy-moving waters of the Tuckahoe Creek have long attracted settlers on its banks from the Nanticoke Indians through Colonial villagers as it flowed into Choptank River. A grist mill operated here in the late 1700s with millstones imported from England.

Frederick Douglass, who escaped slavery and became the abolitionist movement's most eloquent speaker, was born in 1818 on Holmes Hill Farm along the banks of the Tuckahoe. Harriet Tubman was rumored to have established a number of safe houses on the Underground Railroad along the river.

The mill was destroyed in 1924 when a dam burst and was never rebuilt. The State of Maryland began acquiring land along the Tuckahoe in 1962 and the park opened to the public in 1975. Today Tuckahoe State Park contains 3,800 acres of land in the stream valley.

Caroline/Queen Anne's

Phone Number
- (410) 820-1668

Website
- www.dnr.state.md.us/public-lands/eastern/tuckahoe.html

Admission Fee
- Yes, for the Adkins Arboretum

Directions
- From the US 50/301 split on the Eastern Shore, bear to the right on US 50. Make a left at Route 404. Go approximately 8 miles and make a left on MD 480. To your immediate left take Eveland Road to the park.

The Walks

The backbone of a potpourri of canine hiking is the *Tuckahoe Valley Trail* that travels 4.5 easy miles through a climax deciduous forest. The route is well-hydrated with tiny streams. For more varied terrain try the *CreekSide Cliff Trail* that explores the high banks cut by the Tuckahoe. Grab a map and combine the many short trails to craft a canine hiking day - and keep a lookout for evidence of the many settlements that populated the valley over the centuries.

The best place to take your dog at Tuckahoe, however, is the 400-acres of the Adkins Arboretum in the center of the park. Dogs aren't often welcome in these living museums and this one is a real treat. The well-groomed trails work the upland forests around three creeks and after wandering under towering tulip poplars and loblolly pines your dog can luxuriate in the grassy paths of two meadows.

Trail Sense: Trail maps are available and the trails are blazed.

Dog Friendliness
Dogs are allowed throughout the park and in the campground except on the *Lake Trail*.
Traffic
You will encounter bike and equestrian trail users in places but never so much as to feel crowded.
Canine Swimming
Tuckahoe Creek is better suited for splashing and while dogs aren't allowed in the recreation area of Crouse Mill Pond she can get a good swim at the boat ramp.
Trail Time
A full day of canine hiking is possible at Tuckahoe.

"A bone to the dog is not charity.
Charity is the bone shared with the the dog,
when you are just as hungry as the dog."
-Jack London

3

Robert E. Lee Park

The Park

Lake Roland was created in 1862 as Baltimore's first city water reservoir, eventually named for Roland Run, a feeder stream from the north that got its name from 17th-century settler Roland Thornberry. The water system was abandoned in 1915 due to silting in the lake. In the 1940s the 456-acre property was converted into a Baltimore city park (although outside the city limits) using funds bequeathed to the city for a statue honoring Confederate General Robert E. Lee.

Baltimore County

Phone Number
- None

Website
- None

Admission Fee
- None

Directions
- The park is just north of Baltimore and run by the city. The obscured entrance to Robert E. Lee Park is on Lakeside Drive off Falls Road (MD 25), just north of Lake Avenue.

The Walks

Robert E. Lee Park lacks a public entrance, has no signage, no amenities - in short, a perfect place to take a dog. And you will see more dogs per hour here than anywhere in Baltimore. Improvements will mean more visitation and more restrictions on dogs. Until that time, however, Robert E. Lee can provide just about any type of outing you want with your dog.

Interested in a quick walk with a swim? Circle the old Lakeside Park loop above the Lake Roland dam. Looking for a long, solitary hike? Cross the light rail line and explore a maze of hard-packed dirt trails through the woods. Some push into marshy areas along the lake for a bit of Baltimore's best bird watching. Warblers, ducks, geese and herons ply the reed-choked wetlands. Desire a walk around a lake? Cut across the lake on a narrow path beside the rail line (not for skittery dogs - a passing train will be only a few unfenced feet from the trail) and pick up a rollercoaster lakeside path across Lake Roland. Your dog will delight in bounding up the short slopes in happy anticipation of what the other side holds.

Trail Sense: There are no wayfinding aids whatsoever in Robert E. Lee Park.

Dog Friendliness

As dog-friendly a municipal park as a dog owner is likely to find, Robert E. Lee is the unoffical Baltimore dog park.

Traffic

Bikes are allowed on the trails but are far outnumbered by dogs.

Canine Swimming

There are many great places for a canine swim in Lake Roland on the dam side of the railroad bridge; across the tracks access to the lake is more limited. Look for a dip in the wide, but shallow, Jones Falls over here.

Trail Time

More than an hour.

*"No one appreciates the very special genius of
your conversation as a dog does."*
-Christopher Morley

4

Susquehanna State Park

The Park

The first European to set eyes on the Susquehanna River was English explorer John Smith. He was suitably impressed. "Heaven and earth seemed never to have agreed better to frame a place for man's commodious and delightful habitation," he wrote. While sailing in this area, Smith met the native Susquehannocks, who gave the river, the longest of any waterway on the East Coast, its name. Industry came early to the area - the Lapidium community in the park traces its beginnings to 1683 and the park's restored Rock Run Grist Mill dates to 1794. The water-powered mill grinds corn into meal on summer weekends.

Today Susquehanna State Park, opened in 1965, encompasses 2,500 inviting acres.

Harford

Phone Number
- (410) 557-7994

Website
- www.dnr.state.md.us/ publiclands/central/ susquehanna.html

Admission Fee
- There is a $2 admission to the private Steppingstone Museum in the park.

Directions
- The park is 3 miles northwest of Havre de Grace. Take I-95 to MD 155, Exit 89. Go west on MD 155 to MD 161. Turn right and right again on Rock Run Road to the park.

The Walks

Susquehanna State Park is a winning combination of history, scenery and wildlife. The well-maintained trails are short enough to complete and challenging without being exhausting. The abundance of large rocks in the Susquehanna River enables you to sit out in the water while your dog splashes around you. Among its 15 miles of trails the park features several loop trails in the hills above the Susquehanna River Valley. Most are around two miles in distance. If using the green-blazed *Deer Creek Trail* be on the look-out for a magnificent spreading white oak in the middle of the walk. Be aware that there are few streams on the slopes to refresh your dog on a hot day.

The *Lower Susquehanna Heritage Greenways Trail*, which connects the park at Deer Creek with the Conowingo Dam is as pleasant a hike as you can take with your dog. Tracing the route of the 160-year old Susquehanna and Tidewater Canal towpath, the wide dirt path stretches 2.2 shaded miles along the water.

Trail Sense: The trails are well-blazed and easy to follow. A detailed trail map is also available.

Dog Friendliness
Dogs are permitted everywhere in the park, including the campground, except the Deer Creek picnic area.

Traffic
The Susquehanna trails are popular with mountain bikers and equestrians but it is easy to find solitude, especially in the hills.

Canine Swimming
The rock-strewn Susquehanna is full of clear pools for your dog to paddle around in with many points of access from the trail. Be alert for water releases from the Conowingo Dam, however, which make the lower Susquehanna rise dangerously.

Trail Time
More than an hour.

Your dog will find plenty of good swimming in the Susquehanna River.

5
Harpers Ferry National Historic Park

The Park

No place in Maryland packs as much scenic wonder and historical importance into such a small area as Harpers Ferry National Historic Park where the Shenandoah and Potomac rivers join forces. George Washington surveyed here as a young man. Thomas Jefferson hailed the confluence as "one of the most stupendous scenes in Nature" and declared it worth a trip across the Atlantic Ocean just to see. Meriwether Lewis prepared for the Corps of Discovery in 1804 by gathering supplies of arms and military stores at Harpers Ferry. A United States Marine Colonel named Robert E. Lee captured abolitionist John Brown at Harpers Ferry when he attempted to raid the United States Arsenal and arm a slave insurrection. General Thomas "Stonewall" Jackson scored one of his greatest military victories here during the Civil War.

Washington
Phone Number - (304) 535-6029
Website - www.nps.gov/hafe/
Admission Fee - None on the Maryland side
Directions - To reach Maryland Heights, take the last left off of Route 340 before crossing the Potomac River. Turn right on Sandy Hook Road and continue to the parking area across from Harpers Ferry along the C & O Canal.

Congress appropriated funds for a national monument in Harpers Ferry in 1944 and 2,300 acres of Maryland, Virginia and West Virginia were interwoven into the National Historic Park in 1963.

The Walks

Dogs are welcome in Harpers Ferry National Historic Park and hikes are available for every taste and fitness level. On the Maryland side of the Potomac River is the towpath for the Chesapeake & Ohio Canal; the trail is wide, flat and mostly dirt.

Beside the canal, the Maryland Heights rise dramatically 1,448 feet above the rivers. The *Stone Fort Trail* up the Heights is the park's most strenuous hike and one of the most historic. With the outbreak of the Civil War, the Union

Army sought to fortify the strategic Maryland Heights with its commanding views of the waters and busy railroad lines below. The roads leading to the summit were remembered by Union soldiers as "very rocky, steep and crooked and barely wide enough for those wagons."

Wayside exhibits help canine hikers appreciate the effort involved in dragging guns, mortar and cannon up the mountainside. One 9-inch Dahlgren gun capable of lobbing 100-pound shells weighed 9,700 pounds. The trail leads to the remnants of the Stone Fort which straddles the crest of Maryland Heights at its highest elevation.

You walk your dog across the Potomac River bridge - there is open grating that can intimidate skittish dogs - to Lower Town in Harpers Ferry. Here you will find Virginus Island and the ruins of a thriving industrial town that finally succumbed to flooding in 1889. The trails that weave through the ruins are flat and shady and connect to the trails in historic Lower Town, where John Brown barricaded himself in the town's fire engine house and battled Federal troops. Climbing up the steep grade out of Lower Town is a short trail to Jefferson Rock, where Thomas Jefferson recorded his impressions in 1783.

Trail Sense: There are wonderful maps that help diffuse a potentially confusing tri-state area.

Dog Friendliness
Dogs are welcome in Harpers Ferry.
Traffic
There won't be many trail users in Maryland Heights but your dog will need to be well-socialized in Lower Town.
Canine Swimming
There is some access to the Shenandoah River but this outing with your dog will be for walking, not swimming.
Trail Time
You can spend an entire day enjoying Harpers Ferry with your dog.

6
Downs Memorial Park

The Park

In the early days of English settlement Bodkin Neck was the property of land speculators. It came under cultivation in 1828 when Henry Dunbar purchased most of the peninsula. The land that would become Downs Park was lumbered until the mid-1800s and eventually cultivated to grow vegetables on Deer Park Farm. In 1913 the property was purchased by H.R. Mayo Thom who converted his now Rocky Beach Farm - named for the red sandstone thrusting out of the sandy beach - into a gentleman's summer estate.

Anne Arundel

Phone Number
- (410) 222-6230

Website
- web.aacpl.lib.md.us/rp/parks/dp/

Admission Fee
- There is a $4 daily vehicle charge; closed on Tuesdays

Directions
- Downs Park is in Pasadena. Take Pinehurst Road off Mountain Road (MD 177).

The Walks

A paved perimeter trail loops 3.6 miles around the Downs Park property. Most of the twisting route is easy hiking through woodlands of oak and maple and holly and gum. There are another three miles of unpaved trails through the Natural Area, including an eco-trail with interpretive sites. Many of these natural paths are old farm roads - wide and soft under paw.

Trail Sense: A park map is available and the trails are well-marked.

Dog Friendliness

Downs Park is one of the most dog-friendly parks in Maryland. A dog drinking bowl is chained to a water fountain and there is a "pet parking" stall outside the Information Center. Dogs are not allowed to walk through the formal Mother's Garden.

Traffic

The trails in the Natural Area are less crowded than the active recreation sections of the park.

Canine Swimming

Behind the North Overlook is an isolated, scruffy 40-yard stretch of sand known as Dog Beach just for canine aquatics. There is excellent wave action from the Chesapeake Bay and enough sand for digging. For less adventurous dogs there is swimming in a quiet pond adjacent to Dog Beach.

Trail Time

More than an hour.

7
Sugarloaf Mountain

The Park

To geologists Sugarloaf is called a monadnock, a mountain that stands alone, made of tougher stuff than the land that erodes around it. Here that hard rock is quartzite that has survived 14 million years relatively intact.

Free-standing mountains like Sugarloaf - so named because it is said to have resembled loaves of sugar to early settlers - have always fascinated nature lovers. You are driving along in flat farmlands and suddenly, bang, there it is, like an escapee from the nearest mountain range twenty miles away.

That is what happened to Gordon Strong, a wealthy Chicago businessman, who became captivated by Sugarloaf Mountain on a bicycle trip in 1902. He and his wife Louise began acquiring tracts of land on the mountain to preserve it for the enjoyment of the public. In 1924 he consulted with Frank Lloyd Wright to construct a monument of a building on the summit that would be an automobile destination for millions to enjoy the mountain. Wright designed an innovative spiral building that would complement the twisting road by Strong ultimately rejected the plan in favor of a traditional park. Wright used his sketches for the Guggenheim Museum.

During the Franklin Roosevelt administration Interior Secretary Harold Ickes tried to purchase Sugarloaf as a Presidential retreat but Strong - a Republican - would not sell and the search moved to Camp David to the northwest. Instead Gordon Strong set up a private foundation, Stronghold, to manage the mountain for the enjoyment of the public - free of charge. A rare gift indeed.

Frederick

Phone Number
- (301) 874-2024

Website
- www.sugarloafmd.com/index.html

Admission Fee
- None

Directions
- Follow Route I-270 South to the Hyattstown exit, follow MD 109 to Comus, then right on Comus Road to the Stronghold entrance.

The Walks

How would you like to enjoy the views and forests of Sugarloaf Mountain with your dog.? Just about any way you can think of has been anticipated. For

Bonus
Unless you are a guest you can't stop and admire Strong Mansion or its neighbor, Westwood, but you can drive s-l-o-w-l-y past on your way off the mountain.

the canine hiker who is looking for a long ramble around the mountain before heading to the top there are three mostly concentric routes available at different elevations. The longest, typically reserved for equestrians and mountain bikers, is the _Saddleback Horse Trail_ at seven miles. The popular _Northern Peaks Trail_, marked in blue, is a good workout that leaves the casual visitors at the overlooks

This east-looking view is one of many for your dog to enjoy on Sugarloaf Mountain.

and covers five miles. Closest to the summit is the white-blazed _Mountain Loop Trail_ that gains about 400 feet in elevaion across 2.5 miles.

None of these hiking loops actually reach the 1,282-foot summit - that is left to short - but steep - trails from the overlooks. Of the trio of trails that tag the top of Sugarloaf Mountain the _A.M. Thomas Trail_ is the easiest (it uses stone steps) and the _Sunrise Trail_ the steepest; it goes almost straight up in places and your dog's four-wheel drive will come in handy across near-vertical rocks. You may even need to supply some steadying support.

Trail Sense: You can pick up a trail map at the entrance and the trails are well-marked.

Dog Friendliness
Dogs are permitted to enjoy these trails.
Traffic
A quarter million people a year visit Sugarloaf Mountain - but luckily only a small fraction set out on the trails around the mountain.
Canine Swimming
Hiking only; no swimming for your dog.
Trail Time
An hour if you only plan to hike with your dog on the summit area trails but a good half-day if you take advantage of the circuit trails.

33

8

Assateague National Seashore

The Park

The first European settlers - a band of four men - came to Assateague in 1688. At times more than 200 people survived on the shifting sands, fishing or clamming or growing what crops they could. In 1833 the first lighthouse was built but ships still ran aground, including the *Dispatch*, the official yacht of five American presidents. The cruiser was ruined beyond repair when it reached the shore unscheduled on October 10, 1891.

Assateague was connected to the mainland until 1933 when an August hurricane tore open an inlet to the Sinepuxent Bay that now separates Assateague from Ocean City. A bridge to the mainland opened in 1962 and in 1965 Assateague Island became a national seashore.

The Walks

Dogs are not allowed on the three short channel-side nature trails and can not go on lifeguarded beaches but that leaves miles of wide, sandy beaches to hike on with your dog any time of the year.

Worcester

Phone Number
- (410) 641-1441

Website
- www.nps.gov/asis

Admission Fee
- Yes, good for 7 days

Directions
- Assateague's north entrance is at the end of MD 611, eight miles south of Ocean City. When coming on to the island turn right and avoid going straight into the state park. No dogs allowed there.

You can see pawprints like these on the national seashore all year round.

Drive to the furthest parking lot from the entrance gate and head up the boardwalk across the dunes. Make a right and ahead of you will stretch hours of unspoiled canine hiking in the surf and sand. Although the national seashore is within a few hours' drive of tens of million of Americans don't be surprised if you have most of this beach to yourself and your dog - especially in the off-season.

Trail Sense: Walk down the beach in one direction and come back in the other.

Dog Friendliness

Dogs are not allowed in the state park at the northern end of the island but can go on the beach in the national seashore and stay in the campground.

Traffic

As you go south down the beach you will be sharing the beach mostly with surf fishermen.

Canine Swimming

Absolutely - but pack your own sticks for the dog; not much driftwood stays on the beach.

Trail Time

As much or as little as your dog wants on the sand.

Your dog will find 37 miles of soft, sandy beach like this at Assateague.

9
Swallow Falls
State Park

The Park

Early Americans were extremely adept at clearing land for farms and stripping forests for building houses. By 1900, out of five trees that stood east of the Mississippi in Colonial days, only one survived. It was highly unusual to see any big tree in Maryland that had escaped a logger's saw, unless it was too costly to reach.

That was the case with the grove of white pines and hemlocks at Swallow Falls. The giants are the oldest in Maryland - some trees are estimated to be 360 years old. Philanthropist Henry Krug refused to allow the trees to be logged in the gorge and when a World War I plan to dam the Youghiogheny River fell through their suvival was assured.

America's most famous car campers of the early 20th century - industrialists Henry Ford, Thomas Edison and Harvey Firestone camped here at Muddy Creek Falls and during the Depression the Civilian Conservation Corps created the campsite enjoyed by thousands today.

Garrett

Phone Number
- (301) 387-6938

Website
- www.dnr.state.md.us/publiclands/western/swallowfalls.html

Admission Fee
- None

Directions
- From I-68 take Exit 14 at Keysers Ridge and go south on Route 219 for 19.5 miles to Mayhew Inn Road (2 miles past Deep Creek). Turn right on Mayhew Inn Road, travel 4.5 miles to end of road. At the stop sign turn left onto Oakland Sang Run Road, travel 0.3 miles to first road on the right which will be Swallow Falls Road. Turn right and travel 1.3 miles to the park.

The Walks

This is the best single-trail park in Maryland. The *Falls Trail* is easy going for your dog through the river canyon under cool, dark hemlocks. Muddy Creek Falls, Maryland's highest single water plunge at 53 feet, arrives quickly on your canine hike and shortly you arrive at the confluence of Muddy Creek and the Youghiogheny River. Here you'll travel past several

At Swallow Falls come for the hiking; stay for the swimming.

more hydrospectaculars before turning for home. This gorgeous loop covers about one mile.

If your dog is hankering for more trail time there is a 5.5-mile out-and-back trail to Herrington Manor State Park (no dogs allowed). You'll get more water views and more giant hemlocks - be advised that this canine hike involves a stream crossing that may not be doable in times of high water.

Trail Sense: Navigating the Falls Trail is a simple matter.

Dog Friendliness
Dogs are not allowed in the day-use area the Saturday before Memorial Day through Labor Day. Dogs are allowed in the surrounding Potomac and Garrett State Forests anytime. Dogs are also allowed in the campground.

Traffic
Foot traffic only - and plenty of it, but most of the 200,000 annual visitors come in the summer when dogs aren't allowed on the trail.

Canine Swimming
There are some very scenic doggie swimming holes beneath the several falls in the park.

Trail Time
Depends on how long you linger at the plunging waters.

10
Gunpowder Falls State Park –Hereford

The Park

Gunpowder Falls State Park embraces more than 17,000 acres of property in distinct tracts from the Maryland-Pennsylvania state line to the Chesapeake Bay. The Hereford Area on the Big Gunpowder River preserves 3,620 acres of pristine Maryland woodlands. Located where rivers tumble down the fall line of the Piedmont Plateau to the flat Coastal Plain, there was plenty of water power here to drive the industry of a young America. Ruins of these mills, including a gunpowder mill which exploded on the Panther Branch on July 7, 1874, can still be seen in the park.

Baltimore

Phone Number
- (410) 592-2897

Website
- www.dnr.state.md.us/publiclands/hereford.html

Admission Fee
- None

Directions
- The park is near the town of Hereford, one of the county's oldest. Take Exit 27 off I-83 onto Mt. Carmel Road. The main lot is at the end of Bunker Hill Road off York Road. Other trailheads are on Mt. Carmel, York, Masemore, Falls and Big Falls roads.

The Walks

At Hereford the canine hiker can find any length or type of hike to set tails wagging. The marquee trail among 20 miles of hiking is the 7.1-mile *Gunpowder South Trail* that includes bites of trail more reminiscent of West Virginia than Baltimore, especially the western segment from Falls Road to Prettyboy Dam. While most of the narrow dirt trails at Hereford are easy on the paw, this waterside path is rocky and requires a fair amount of rock scrambling. Your reward is stunning views of the rugged gorge. Walking along the *South Trail*, and its companion *North Trail* on the opposite bank, is generally level as it follows the meanderings of the stream. For hearty climbers, look to the many side trails which can be wedded to the *South Trail* to form several loops of between one and two miles of length.

Trail Sense: The *South Trail* is blazed in white and most side trails are blazed in blue. Equestrian trails are blazed yellow. Trail maps are available but not on site; consult the mapboard in the York Road parking lot in the middle of the park.

Dog Friendliness
Dogs are allowed on all the trails but not in the campground at Camp Wood.

Traffic
Most of the traffic you see will be out in the river.

Canine Swimming
Although limited by high banks, fisherman and watercraft, there are plenty of great pools in the Big Gunpowder Falls. Two favorites are at the confluence of the Panther Branch and the Big Gunpowder and beneath an imposing outcropping just downstream from Raven Falls.

Trail Time
More than an hour.

Your dog will forget he is in the Baltimore suburbs
during a day at Gunpowder - Hereford.

II
Rock Creek Regional Park

The Park

In 1965 an earthen dam was built creating Lake Needwood to prevent small stream flooding and control sediment. In 1967 another earthen dam was constructed down the road on the north branch of Rock Creek to create Lake Bernard Frank for the same reasons. Together the two lakes are the centerpieces of the 2,700-acre Rock Creek Regional Park.

The Walks

The two sections of Rock Creek Regional Park each radiate different personalities. Lake Needwood is a bit more rough-and-tumble with picnic shelters on the shore and boaters - including an outboard powered pontoon

Montgomery

Phone Number
- (301) 948-5053

Website
- www.mc-mncppc.org/parks/
facilities/regional_parks/
rockcreek/index.shtm

Admission Fee
- None

Directions
- The park segments are located northeast of Rockville and Gaithersburg. From Norbeck Road (MD 28) take Muncaster Mill Road west. Lake Frank and Meadowside Nature Center are on the left; Lake Needwood is down on Needwood Road.

boat that cruises the lake on weekends - out on the water. The most-favored route for canine hikers here is a trip around the 75-acre lake partly on an old access road and partly on dirt paths. This is a shady, sometimes hilly circuit that hugs the shoreline and gives your dog plenty of opportunity for a swim.

Lake Frank is given over to quiet, passive recreation. Aside from fishing on the lake the primary activity to take place here is hiking. Eight miles of well-maintained trails spread out from the Meadowside Nature Center. To stretch your dog's legs you can tour Lake Frank for over three miles on the *Lakeside Trail* or for those hounds with short attention spans you can jump from trail to trail on the many short, themed paths.

There are many delights to found around the corners here: an old mill site, a restored log cabin, and even a covered bridge built by Rockville High School students. On the natural side your dog will wander through rock formations and past surging streams and hidden ponds.

Trail Sense: Trail maps are available for both Lake Needwood and Lake Frank. The Meadowside Nature Center map is a model of its kind.

Dog Friendliness

Dogs are welcome on all Rock Creek trails, including those of the nature center.

Traffic

This is a busy place but you can usually get away on a side trail.

Canine Swimming

If you don't disturb the year-round fishermen your dog can enjoy some excellent dog paddling.

Trail Time

You can use the park for a short nature hike or take advantage of many hours of varied canine hiking.

Rocks at Rock Creek? Who would have guessed.

12
Fair Hill
NRMA

The Park

William du Pont Jr., great grandson of the founder of the chemical giant, built a sporting empire in Delaware that spilled over the state line into Fair Hill. He operated Foxcather Farms, stabling five Kentucky Derby starters over the years. His horse farm at Fair Hill covered more than 5,000 acres and was one of the largest private land holdings in the East.

Fair Hill was purchased by the State of Maryland in 1975 and the equestrian trappings of the farm have survived intact, including an active steeplechase course and stable that was home to 2006 Kentucky Derby champion Barbaro.

Cecil

Phone Number
- (410) 398-1246

Website
- www.dnr.state.md.us/public-lands/central/fairhill.html

Admission Fee
- A daily parking fee on the honor system

Directions
- Take Exit 100 off I-95 toward Rising Sun on MD 272 North. Take a right on MD 273 and follow to the intersection of MD 273 and MD 213. There are five major parking areas; turn right to the office.

The Walks

This is the Godzilla of area hiking. Traversing its 5,613 acres are over 75 miles of natural, multi-use trails. Many go through rolling hayfields as befits its stature as a leading equine training center. Most of the trails in Maryland are heavily forested and if you like the feel of sunshine on your face and long hikes across open fields Fair Hill is the place to bring your dog.

The trails through the fields are typically doubletrack (old dirt vehicle roads). Singletrack trails dominate in the forested areas. The stiffest climbs are in the vicinity of the Big Elk Creek but most of the trails are like walking a steeplechase course. Fair Hill is also a good place to spot house ruins along the trail.

The Big Elk Creek surges through the property and is spanned by many trail bridges, including one of Maryland's five remaining covered bridges. The

Big Elk Creek Covered Bridge was built in 1860 at a cost of $1,165.00. When it was reconstructed in 1992 after sustaining extensive damage from heavy trucks, the tab was $152,000.

Trail Sense: Most trails are not marked and there are times you can feel like a real explorer when you leave the doubletrack trails. Unless you enjoy that feeling all day, a trail map from the office is mandatory. Be aware - there are more dead ends here than in an English maze garden.

Dog Friendliness
Dogs are welcome on the Fair Hill trails.

Traffic
Mountain bikes are allowed on the trails and, of course, horses but you will most certainly find plenty of elbow room here.

Canine Swimming
If your dog loves a good swim pick a trail near the Big Elk Creek.

Trail Time
Many, many, many hours of trail time here.

13
Soldiers Delight
NEA

The Park

Soldiers Delight NEA's 1900 acres are part of a prairie-like grassland that rests on igneous rock that is one of only three such formations in North America. Early settlers called the area of Blackjack Pines and Post Oaks "The Barrens" because its low nutrient level was unfriendly to cultivation. The distinctive green rock was named "serpentine" for its resemblance to a snake native to northern Italy. This arid soil has produced a landscape more common in the American West than suburban Baltimore. Here you will find rare insects, rocks and at least 39 endangered plant species.

Baltimore

Phone Number
- (410) 922-3044

Website
- dnr.state.md.us/publiclands/central/soldiers.html

Admission Fee
- None

Directions
- Soldiers Delight is west of Owings Mills. From I-795 take Franklin Boulevard West to Church Road. Go right and left on Berrymans Lane and left on Deer Park Road to the Visitor Center on the right.

The Walks

The thing that makes Soldiers Delight so unique and visually appealing - the serpentine barrens - does not do hiking dogs any favors. The green-tinted stone is embedded in probably half of the park's seven miles of trails, jutting through the soil in hard ridges. So little soil accumulates in the barrens that the Maryland Geological Survey locates its seismic recording station here because such ready access to the bedrock makes it a simple matter to record vibrations during earthquakes. Soldiers Delight, so easy on the eye, can be tough on the paw.

The trail system is essentially two loops connected at the Deer Park Road Overlook, While the terrain rolls up and down there are no tough climbs on these hikes. The woods are airy - and will become more so. The Virginia pines and Eastern Red Cedar you see are invasive species being removed by prescribed burning.

Trail Sense: The well-marked trails are shown own a trail map.

Dog Friendliness
Dogs are permitted throughout Soldiers Delight.

Traffic
The trails are for hikers and are seldom crowded.

Canine Swimming
Swimming is limited at Soldiers Delight; Red Run (on the *Dolfield and Red Run Trails*) and Chimney Branch (on the *Serpentine Trail*) are rarely knee-high to a dogleg.

Trail Time
A few hours to complete these trails.

14

Paw Paw Tunnel

The Park

The biggest obstacle to the completion of the Chesapeake and Ohio Canal was five miles of crooked Potomac River water known as the Paw Paw Bends. It was decided to by-pass the curves with a tunnel, destined to be the largest man-made structure on the 184-mile canal.

Rosy-eyed planners began work on the tunnel in 1836 with a goal of 7-8 feet gained a day. Instead, the pace was more like 12 feet a week. Fourteen years later - with a cost overrun of 500% - the 26-foot high tunnel was opened.

Allegany

Phone Number
- (301) 678-5463

Website
- www.nps.gov/choh

Admission Fee
- None

Directions
- Take I-70 to Hancock and go south on Route 522 to Berkeley Springs, West Virginia. Turn west on Route 9 and go 28 miles to Paw Paw.

Encased in the six million bricks used to build the Paw Paw Tunnel at Mile 155 are tales of unpaid wages, immigrant worker abuse, labor unrest and even murder. The canal finally closed in 1924 after several devastating floods crippled commerce on the waterway.

The Walks

This is the most unique hike you can take with your dog in Maryland. The first thing you need to know is bring a flashlight - there are no lights in the tunnel and it is long enough to envelop you in complete darkness.

This canine hike starts in a national park service campground and travels a short distance on the well-maintained towpath of the canal until you reach the Paw Paw Tunnel. At this point you can plunge directly into the 3,118-foot tunnel (more than a half-mile long) or veer to your right and lead your dog on a hardy hike over the top of the tunnel on the *Tunnel Hill Trail*. You will rejoin the towpath on the opposite side of the tunnel and complete your loop by returning through the darkness.

Trail Sense: The *Tunnel Hill Trail* is blazed in orange and they do come in handy; the towpath is self-explanatory.

Dog Friendliness
Dogs are allowed on the trails along the C&O Canal and in the surrounding Green Ridge State Forest. Dogs are also allowed in the campground.

Traffic
Bikes are allowed on the towpath but don't expect to find anyone else in the tunnel.

Canine Swimming
There is access to the Potomac River at a canoe launch for excellent dog swims.

Trail Time
It will take about an hour to fully explore the Paw Paw Tunnel.

Heading west into the Paw Paw Tunnel...

...and passing on through.

15

Gunpowder Falls State Park–Sweet Air

The Park

Unlike other sections of Gunpowder Falls State Park, the water is not the star at Sweet Air. Only a short segment of the trail system follows the Little Gunpowder Falls, which flows thinly near its headwaters at this point. The attraction at Sweet Air is a patchwork of open fields (still under cultivation) and wooded landscapes on either side of the river.

The Walks

Sweet Air offers more than twelve miles of well-marked rambles on four main trails and several connector branches. The feature hike is the white-blazed *Little Gunpowder Trail*, serving up a buffet of Sweet Air splendor in the course of its 3.8 miles: fern-encrusted hillsides, upland farm fields and ultra-green forests. Short loops off this trail visit a quiet woodland pond and a small white pine plantation. Look for a cornucopia of trail surfaces - soft dirt, hard pack, wood chip and mown grass.

A total exploration of Sweet Air will include the blue-blazed *Boundary Trail* which means wading through the Little Gunpowder to walk into Baltimore County. If this proves enjoyable, consider some of the rogue trails at Sweet Air near the water.

Trail Sense: A trail map is available but not on site. In addition to blazed routes there are signposts with "You Are Here" maps indicating shortcuts sprinkled on the trail system.

Baltimore/Harford

Phone Number
- (410) 557-7994

Website
- www.dnr.state.md.uspubliclands/ central/ gunpowder.html

Admission Fee
- None

Directions
- The Sweet Air section is east of Jacksonville. From Sweet Air Road (MD 145) turn onto Greene Road and make a left on Moores Road to park entrance.

Dog Friendliness
Dogs are permitted on the trails at Sweet Air.
Traffic
The trails are popular with equestrians and bikes are permitted but Sweet Air is blissfully uncrowded.
Canine Swimming
Gunpowder Falls is generally deep enough only for sustained splashing but the farm ponds on the property make for good dog paddling.
Trail Time
More than an hour.

"Dogs' lives are too short. Their only fault, really."
-Agnes Sligh Turnbull

16
Oregon Ridge Park

The Park

An active mining community thrived at Oregon Ridge in the mid-19th century. Irish immigrants and emancipated slaves did most of the hard work pulling first Geothite, containing iron ore, and then high-grade Cockeysville marble from the hills. The iron was smelted in a furnace along Oregon Branch and the marble was used to build the United States Capitol and the Washington Monument. The Oregon Ridge Iron Works supported a company town of 220 workers and their families before the business died away in the 1870s. Today Oregon Ridge Park is Baltimore County's largest park with more than 1000 acres of woods and meadows.

Baltimore

Phone Number
- (410) 887-1815

Website
- www.oregonridge.org

Admission Fee
- None

Directions
- Oregon Ridge Park is 2 miles west of Cockeysville. From I-83 take Exit 20B west on Shawan Road. After one mile make a left on Beaver Dam Road and immediately take right fork into the park.

The Walks

Although you get under way with a pleasant stroll into the forest across the wooden bridge spanning the Grand Canyon of Oregon Ridge (an abandoned open pit mine), it doesn't take long to realize you have signed on for a serious hike here. The *Loggers Red Trail* pulls you to the top of the ridge - elevated enough to launch hang gliders - and your pick of nine short trails. The full loop of the property leads south along the yellow trails and will add 4 stream crossings and serious hill climbs to your outing.

All told there are 6 miles of trails at Oregon Ridge. All are wooded and almost uniformly wide and soft to the paw. The lone exception is the rocky slopes of the *S. James Campbell Trail* which are a trade-off for the scenic trekking in the ravine. Be sure to make your way to the half-mile *Lake Trail*, a rollicking romp above the green waters of the 45-foot deep Oregon Lake, a flooded old iron quarry.

Trail Sense: A trail map is available outside the Nature Center, the trails are well-marked and signposts at junctions alert you to new trailheads.

Dog Friendliness

Dogs are allowed throughout the Oregon Ridge Park trail system and if you've forgotten a leash you can borrow one in the Nature Center. Dogs are not permitted in the beach area at Oregon Lake.

Traffic

No horses or bikes are allowed on these trails.

Canine Swimming

Baisman Run is simply for splashing but Ivy Pond at the junction of the *Ivy Hill* and *S. James Campbell* trails is a delightful stop for a dip, ringed by fir trees and outcroppings of Loch Raven schist.

Trail Time

More than an hour.

"The best thing about a man is his dog."
-French Proverb

17
Great Falls
Tavern

The Park

George Washington was one of the early American speculators who dreamed of the riches an inland American waterway could bring that would float goods from the West to Washington down the Potomac River. A canal that could connect the Potomac River to the Ohio River in Pittsburgh would provide a continuous water link from New Orleans to the Cheasapeake Bay.

The canal, dubbed the "Great National Project" by President John Quincy Adams, was finally started on July 4, 1828. It would take 22 years to complete - actually construction just stopped since the canal route never made it out of Maryland with only 184.5 of the planned 460 miles dug - and was obsolete before it opened. Battling the young and ever-improving railroads, the Chesapeake & Ohio Canal lasted for 75 years floating cargo from Cumberland, Maryland to Georgetown. The ditch survived filling in through the efforts of Supreme Court Justice William O. Douglas who championed the canal as "a long stretch of quiet and piece."

Montgomery

Phone Number
- (301) 767-3714

Website
- www.nps.gov/choh/index.

Admission Fee
- Yes, a 3-day pass

Directions
- The park entrance is at the junction of Falls Road (Route 189) and MacArthur Boulevard. Take Exit 39 off I-495 and continue on River Road (Route 190) West before turning left on Falls Road.

The Walks

At the Great Falls Tavern Visitor Center of the Chesapeake & Ohio National Historic Park dogs are denied the extraordinary views of the powerful Great Falls of the Potomac and Mather Gorge - they are banned from the boardwalk trails on the Olmsted Island Bridges and the rock-scrambling on the *Billy Goat "A" Trail* around Bear Island. But canine hikers are welcome everywhere else and park staff even maintains a watering bowl for pets at the Visitor Center drinking fountain. The packed sand and paw-friendly towpath is one of the most scenic of its ilk - the canal section around the Great Falls opens wide and

the boulder-edged water calls to mind the Canadian Rockies rather than suburban Washington.

Away from the Potomac a trail system penetrates the wooded hills above the river. These wide dirt trails make for easy dog walking through an airy, mature forest. The key route is the *Gold Mine Loop* that pushes out from behind the Visitor Center. Various short spur trails, some marked and some not, radiate off the 3.2-mile loop. The *River Trail* above the Washington Aqueduct Dam takes canine hikers along river's edge for about one mile. Even though the water can seem placid at this point, beware of unpredictable currents in the river - the Potomac River has claimed scores of lives over the years.

Trail Sense: The trails are well-marked and a trail map is available.

Dog Friendliness
Canine hikers are welcome everywhere save for the *Billy Goat Trail*.

Traffic
Off the towpath there is often plenty of breathing room in the hills.

Canine Swimming
Along the *River Trail* there are a few spots where it is not too wild and wooly for a cautious dip.

Trail Time
Several hours to a full day if you set out along the towpath.

53

18
Gambrill State Park

The Park

Private individuals with an interest in conservation ushered Gambrill State Park into existence. The land was presented to the City of Frederick on September 7, 1934 to be preserved as a public park on Catoctin Mountain. The City in turn gave the land to the State of Maryland who created the 1,137-acre park. It was named for James H. Gambrill, a Frederick miller and brewer and conservationist who had died in 1932.

Most of the recreational facilities, including three native stone overlooks, were built in the 1930s by workers in the Civilian Conservation Corps.

Frederick

Phone Number
- (301) 271-7574

Website
- www.dnr.state.md.us/public-lands/western/gambrill.html

Admission Fee
- None

Directions
- The park entrance is on Gambrill Park Road off US 40, west of Frederick and the I-70 interchange.

The Walks

Gambrill State Park offers a nicely designed trail system to accommodate any type of hiking outing you are looking for with your dog. All trails begin at the same lot (one mile into the park on the east side of the road) and loop back to your car. Beginners can enjoy the heavily forested mountain top on the *Lost Chestnut* and *Red Maple* trails, each about a mile and, save for one steep descent on the red trail, easy to hike.

For most canine hikers the first option will be the 3.3-mile *Black Locust Trail*. You may not think so as you drop off the mountain on a paw-pounding rocky path and then start back up again but your dog's tail will be wagging again after the trail splits from the 26.5-mile blue-blazed *Catoctin Trail* that is running the length of the mountain. Up ahead are the destinations on this canine hike - overlooks of Frederick to the east and South Mountain to the west. This trail is especially tasty after you cross the road when you burrow through tunnels of mountain laurel.

The springhouse at Bootjack Spring will be your dog's favorite spot on a hot day in Gambrill State Park.

If you are hankering for a full afternoon of canine hiking on Catoctin Mountain take off on the *Yellow Poplar Trail* that keeps to the ridge crest for the most part. This longest of the Gambrill trails is a favorite with mountain bikers.

Trail Sense: There is a one-of-a-kind three-dimensional mapboard at the trailhead but nothing to carry with you. The trails, however, are probably the most enthusiastically blazed in Maryland - there are times it seems the trail maintenance crews haven't missed a tree.

Dog Friendliness
Dogs are permitted on the trails but not in the picnic areas or the Tea Room, the stone lodge in the park.
Traffic
The parking lot holds about 20 cars and is likely to be filled on nice days but there is a surprising amount of open trail on the mountain.
Canine Swimming
Not on Catoctin Mountain.
Trail Time
You can leave after a half-hour trail or spend several hours.

19
Patapsco Valley State Park

The Park

Maryland's state park system began with the establishment of Patapsco State Forest Reserve in 1907. Today the park sprawls across 14,000 acres and four counties. The linear park traces the Patapsco River for 32 miles from southeastern Carroll County to tidewater in Baltimore Harbor.

several counties

Phone Number
- (410) 260-8835

Website
- dnr.state.md.us/publiclands central/patapscovalley.html

Admission Fee
- only in developed areas (where dogs can't go)

Directions
- see The Walks

The Walks

The widespread prohibitions against dogs in developed areas of Patapsco Valley State Park are a prime frustration for Maryland dog owners. But there is plenty of lemonade to be squeezed from the lemons served up by the State of Maryland. Four undeveloped areas are recommended by the park service to take the dog:

Feezer's Lane (*gravel road on west side of Marriottsville Road just north of the bridge over North Branch of Patapsco River*). A narrow trail follows a high bank of the river for about a mile until it reaches a small stream crossing and opens into a burst of hiking opportunities in the Liberty Dam Reservoir. Straight ahead is the base of the Liberty Dam and a deep pool, to the right is a winding trek up a rocky old construction road (not recommended for soft paws) to a park at the top of the dam, to the left are miles of hilly, wooded equestrian trails.

Henryton Road (*off MD 99 at the end of the road at the washed out bridge over South Branch Patapsco River*). An unmarked fisherman's trail follows the stream for miles; it is particularly interesting to the east. The first part is wild and wooly with many fallen trees to clamber over. The slopes are so littered with uprooted giants you may want to keep an eye out for any others about to tumble. Once across the railroad tracks the trail enters a flood plain and becomes buttery soft to the paw, beckoning you to continue. When you begin to hear vehicular traffic, turn around and head back. The best of this hike is over.

Daniels Area (*at end of Daniels Road off Old Frederick Road, east of the intesection of Routes 29 and 99*). Daniels was once a bustling mill village done in by shifting economics and flooding from Hurricane Agnes in 1972. You can enjoy either the flattest dogwalking in greater Baltimore or some of the steepest here. A hiking loop begins just across the small stream by the parking lot; to the left the trail switchbacks to the top of a high ridge past the Camel's Den cave and to the right it begins a 2.5-mile journey on a former railbed of the Baltimore & Ohio Railroad. After exploring the ridge for a mile the high trail drops down to the level riverside walk where you can complete the loop or turn left and follow as the old access road gives way to a single track dirt path. Behind the Daniels Dam, the Patapsco River is wide and still here, giving this walk a feel quite unlike any other in the region.

Hilltop Road at Hilton Area (*off Frederick Road, Md 144, between Catonsville and Ellicott City*). The state park actually offers up a pair of blazed hiking trails to ostracized dog owners in this section of Patapsco State Park above the Bloede Dam, the first hydro-power dam to have electricty-producing turbines inside the dam. The Hilton Area is where John Glenn gave 43 acres of land to start the park nearly a century ago. The main trail at Hilltop is the yellow-blazed *Buzzards Rock Trail*, a 1.7-mile loop. The red-blazed *Sawmill*

Branch Trail can also be used to complete the loop, but you will miss Buzzards Rock itself. This rocky promontory overlooks the tree-lined gorge where you can spot a gliding turkey vulture or just gauge how far you've climbed up or how far you have to go down. This trail up the cliff is steep, hard going but most of the walking through the mature forest at Hilltop or along the river is quite easy.

Trail Sense: These undeveloped areas are not on all park maps. Pick up the flyer A Guide To Your Pet in Patapsco Valley State Park for directions to dog-friendly hiking areas. Once there, the trails are generally not blazed.

Dog Friendliness
Dogs are only allowed in Patapsco State Park in undeveloped areas such as the ones described. Dogs are allowed in the campground at the Hollofield Area (only in about a dozen campsites) but can't leave the campsite.

Traffic
These undeveloped areas are not nearly as crowded as the popular people-only parts of Patapsco State Park.

Canine Swimming
There is great canine swimming in the Patapsco River in all four park areas, save Feezer's Lane. As the Liberty Dam releases no water, this section of the river is all but dry. A deep pool at the base of the dam is tempting but difficult for the dog to access from the shore.

Trail Time
Many hours - or days - are possible on these trails.

"My dog can bark like a Congressman, fetch like an aide, beg like a press secretary and play dead like a receptionist."
-Gerald Solomon

As a young lawyer, 19th century Senator George Graham Vest of Missouri, addressed the jury on behalf of his client, suing a neighbor who had killed his dog. Vest's speech has come to be known as "Tribute to the Dog."

The best friend a man has in the world may turn against him and become his enemy. His son or daughter that he has reared with loving care may prove ungrateful. Those who are nearest and dearest to us, those whom we trust with our happiness and our good name may become traitors to their faith. The money that a man has, he may lose. It flies away from him, perhaps when he needs it most. A man's reputation may be sacrificed in a moment of ill-considered action. The people who are prone to fall on their knees to do us honor when success is with us may be the first to throw the stone of malice when failure settles its cloud upon our heads. The one absolutely unselfish friend that man can have in this selfish world, the one that never deserts him, the one that never proves ungrateful or treacherous is his dog. A man's dog stands by him in prosperity and in poverty, in health and in sickness. He will sleep on the cold ground, where the wintry winds blow and the snow drives fiercely, if only he may be near his master's side. He will kiss the hand that has no food to offer; he will lick the wounds and sores that come in an encounter with the roughness of the world. He guards the sleep of his pauper master as if he were a prince. When all other friends desert, he remains. When riches take wings, and reputation falls to pieces, he is as constant in his love as the sun in its journey through the heavens. If fortune drives the master forth an outcast in the world, friendless and homeless, the faithful dog asks no higher privilege than that of accompanying him, to guard him against danger, to fight against his enemies. And when the last scene of all comes, and death takes his master in its embrace and his body is laid away in the cold ground, no matter if all other friends pursue their way, there by the graveside will the noble dog be found, his head between his paws, his eyes sad, but open in alert watchfulness, faithful and true even in death.

20
Cedarville
State Forest

The Park

The Piscataway Indians came to this area in southern Maryland for winter camps. Later settlers attempted - with varying degrees of success - to drain the swamp for cropland. The Maryland Department of Natural Resources came in 1930 to buy thousands of acres of land for a forest demonstration area. Twenty years later, as the trees grew up, many were harvested to provide charcoal to heat other state properties across Maryland. Today's park encompasses 3,510 acres.

Charles

Phone Number
- (301) 888-1410

Website
- www.dnr.state.md.us/public-lands/southern/cedarville.html

Admission Fee
- Yes, currently $3

Directions
- From US 301 South travel to Cedarville Road. As you leave Prince George's County take a left on Cedarville Road. Make a right on Bee Oak Road, which is the main entrance to the forest.

The Walks

If your dog were to design trails they might look a lot like the four main trails in Cedarville State Forest. Start with packed dirt trails without many rocks and roots. Throw in some paw-friendly sand and pine straw for variety. Make them wide, like the Civilian Conservation Corps did back in the 1930s. Route them along many streams to provide cool refreshment - and don't worry about low-lying spots since what dog doesn't enjoy a bit of mud. And don't include too many of those bothersome steep hills.

The *Holly Trail* is Cedarville's longest at five miles and your dog will get a squishy feel for the marshy areas of the forest as you follow orange blazes. For elevation changes clock in on the 3.5-mile *Heritage Trail*. Here you'll see one of the kilns that churned out as much as 3,600 pounds of charcoal a week.

Two shorter trails can be explored in less than an hour: the *Plantation Trail* takes in a loblolly pine plantation and the *Swamp Trail* loops through the headwaters of Zekiah Swamp. The forest can keep your dog busy with over 19 miles of marked trails.

Trail Sense: The trails are marked with color posts and blazes.

Dog Friendliness

Dogs are allowed throughout Cedarville State Forest and in the campground.

Traffic

All trails are shared with bikes and horses.

Canine Swimming

Numerous streams and springs keep the forest well-lubricated and there is a 4-acre pond at the *Plantation Trail* trailhead.

Trail Time

A short hour to a full day.

Your dog can join the many mushroom hunters who favor the forests of southern Maryland.

21
Gunpowder Falls State Park–Belair Road

The Park

The fall line between the Piedmont and coastal plains occurs in this section of the park, just west of Route 40. Sloops could come up the Big Gunpowder Falls as far as this point to load shipments from the many mills operating upstream. A popular ferry once operated at Long Calm, the stretch of river west of today's I-95. The Marquis de Lafayette camped here famously during the American Revolution. Today the park's trails run for 8 miles along the Big Gunpowder Falls water chutes.

The Walks

The highlight for canine hikers here is the Sweathouse Branch Wildlands Area that provides some of the best loop trails in the Gunpowder park system. The outside loop links the *Wildlands Trail* (pink), the *Stocksdale Trail* (blue) and the *Sweathouse Trail* (yellow) and covers 5.1 miles. The healthy hill climbs and wide trails give a big feel to this walk as it meanders through differing forest types. These trails are rocky under paw at times.

On the east side of U.S. Route 1 the *Lost Pond Trail* runs in a 3.1-mile long lasso on its way to an abandoned mill pond. The yellow-blazed *Sawmill Trail* loops off this footpath into the hillside of the gorge to visit the ruins of the 1833 Carroll family sawmill. These trails require several stream crossings and are often muddy. For all-day hikers the *Big Gunpowder Trail* picks its way through the woods along the entire length of the river on the south bank, eventually reaching

Baltimore

Phone Number
- (410) 557-7994

Website
- www.dnr.state.md.uspubliclands/ central/ gunpowder.html

Admission Fee
- None

Directions
- The parking area and trailheads are on the northbound side of US 1 (Belair Road) after it crosses the Big Gunpowder Falls, about 5.4 miles north of the I-695 Beltway). Polar parking lots on the ends of the park are on the south side of the river on Harford Road (MD 147) and on Jones Road off the Pulaski Highway (US 40).

the last rapids of the Gunpowder. The narrow dirt trail is blazed white.

Trail Sense: A trail map is available at the main park office in Kingsville but not on site. Consult the mapboard in the parking lot to plan routes. The trails are extremely well-marked.

Dog Friendliness

Dogs are allowed on all these trails.

Traffic

Bicycles are banned from the Sweathouse Branch Wildlands Area. While popular, there are many more available miles of trail here than users.

Canine Swimming

Unless recent rains have been heavy, the dam-controlled Big Gunpowder Falls is often only deep enough only for splashing. But on Long Green Run, past the Sweathouse Trail, is one of the best canine swimming holes in the Baltimore area. Racing water is funnelled into a deep pool by a whale-shaped rock that serves as a natural diving board for playful dogs.

Trail Time

A half-day and more is possible.

22
Savage Park

The Park

Amos Williams and three brothers built a cotton works on the Patuxent River in 1822, naming it for John Savage, a director of the Bank of the United States who backed the project with $20,000. A major cloth producer for 125 years, the business declined rapidly after World War II due to a glut of canvas from returning war supplies and was gone by 1947. A visionary named Harry Heim bought the entire company town for $450,000 with dreams of a year-round Christmas village called Santa Heim, Merryland. Perhaps ahead of his time, the scheme suffered a quick death and the old mill was used mainly for warehouses until renovated for shops and offices and a park in 1988.

Howard

Phone Number
- (410) 313-4682

Website
- www.co.ho.md.us/
  rpsavage.html

Admission Fee
- None

Directions
- Savage Park is west of Savage, west of US 1. To reach the Wincopin Trails, exit US 1 to Guilford Road west. Make a left on Vollmerhausen Road to parking lot on left past schools. The Savage Loop is in town at the end of Baltimore Street. Parking for the Savage Mill Trail is on Foundry Street.

The Walks

Three unconnected areas surrounding the confluence of the Middle Patuxent and Little Patuxent rivers conspire to form Savage Park. Although the Wincopin Neck Trails are the prime destination of the canine hiker, you may want to warm up on the *Savage Historic Mill Trail*. This wide, level wooded path traces the boulder-pocked stream below the confluence for 3/4 of a mile. Pools in the falls are the prettiest canine swimming holes in the Baltimore region. Up the road are the hilly *River Trail* and *Lost Horse Trail* behind the recreation area.

The main hiking routes at Wincopin Neck are the red-blazed *Wincopin Trail* and the green-blazed *Beech Grove Trail*. The Wincopin heads straight out from the parking lot before plunging downhill to loop around Hogs Neck in the Middle Patuxent River; the Beech Grove circles to the left and down to the Little Patuxent River. Most hiking is along wide pathways, save for rocky and narrow stretches near the Middle Patuxent. The walks are surprisingly flat except for steep descents to the shoreline.

Not so flat is the short, yellow-blazed *Pick Rock Loop*, which charges down the hill to the river and back. A 1.5-mile white-blazed spur here leaves the I-95 bridge along a wooded ridge. If you choose, at the end of this out-and-back trail you can return on overgrown deer trails in the stream valley along the river.

Trail Sense: The trails are blazed and a there is a mapboard.

Dog Friendliness
Dogs are permitted on all the Savage Park trails.

Traffic
The park is generally lightly used.

Canine Swimming
There is ample opportunity for dog paddling at Savage Park, the best coming in the Middle Patuxent River where access is easiest.

Trail Time
Several hours across the entire park.

23

Rachel Carson Conservation Park

The Park

The park remembers the work of Rachel Louise Carson, a product of southern Pennsylvania farms who lived in Silver Spring. After her schooling Carson came to Baltimore to study and teach at Johns Hopkins and eventually she joined the zoology department at the University of Maryland.

She indulged a lifelong love of the sea by leaving for a post with the Bureau of Fisheries in Washington as an aquatic biologist in 1936. She began writing and editing for the government before leaving to write about biology fulltime in 1952. By this time she had gained world fame with the award-winning book, *The Sea Around Us*.

Montgomery

Phone Number
- None

Website
- www.mc-mncppc.org/parks/park_maps/map_pages/rachel-carsoncp/rachelcarsoncp.shtm

Admission Fee
- None

Directions
- The park is in Brookeville. Take New Hampshire Avenue (Route 650) past Georgia Avenue (Route 97) and make a left on Sundown Road. Turn left on Zion Road and parking is on the left.

Her seminal work, *Silent Spring*, was published a decade later and introduced Americans to the dangers inherent in widespread use of chemical pesticides. Rachel Carson died of breast cancer shortly thereafter and is buried in Rockville, just south of the conservation area.

The Walks

There is a lot for your dog to love about Rachel Carson Conservation Park. First, it is close enough to Washington and Baltimore that you can get there without having your dog bounce around the car for hours but not so close to civilization that the trails are clogged with locals taking their dogs out for a quick 15-minute spin. Second, the terrain rolls just enough to keep your dog's interest without setting tongues to panting. Third, there is a nice mix of grassy, open-field canine hiking to soak in the sunshine and shady woods. Toss in some scenic rock-outcroppings and the gurgling meanderings of the Hawlings River (if you have never wondered what the difference is between a creek and a river you will when you see the Hawlings. The difference? There is no official definition; just a perception by the naming agency).

The 650 acres of the park were settled by Quaker farmers who were gentle stewards of the land. The mature chestnut oak forest is one of the best examples of its type in Maryland but before you reach the woods your dog can enjoy the grassy trails of the *Equestrian Loop*. If your dog has a taste for the grass under paw down the ways on Zion Road is the 1.25-mile *Blue Mash Nature Trail*, favored by birders.

Your canine hiking day at Rachel Carson Conservation Area begins on these wide, grassy paths.

Trail Sense: There is a mapboard at the parking lot but this is the kind of park you study the trail map after you finish the hike and say, "So that's where we were." The blue blazes you encounter for a short time in the woods are to indicate that the trail is hiker-only. There are signs at junctions throughout the park pointing you back to the trailhead.

Dog Friendliness
Dogs are welcome across the park.
Traffic
Extremely light; no bikes are allowed but these are horse trails.
Canine Swimming
The Hawlings River is best suited for splashing.
Trail Time
Several hours.

24

American Chestnut Land Trust

The Park

In 1986 local landowners banded together to protect their community from approaching development. Largely by digging deep into their own pockets, they put together $500,000 to help purchase two threatened tracts of land totaling 441 acres. Subsequent acquisitions have pushed the trust holdings to 810 acres. The mandate for the organization has expanded to the protection of open space around Parkers Creek - the last undeveloped creek on the western shore of the Chesapeake Bay - and they manage another 1,770 acres.

The Walks

These natural, hiker-only trails are sure to set any dog's tail to wagging. If you only have time for a visit to one of the two hiking tracts serious canine hikers and water-loving dogs will favor the steep hills and trails along Parkers Creek of the Double Oak Farm Tract. The trail of choice for most will be the three-mile *Parkers Creek Loop* but the adventurous may want to test the out-and-back Goldstein Bay Farm Trail. Expect patches of unsure footing under paw and steep hills on this three-mile round trip.

The Gravatt Tract features three distinct loops. The *Ridge Loop* and sections of the *Stream Loop* (it no longer loops thanks to an active beaver community) visit wetlands and old homesteads. The *Laurel Loop* is an early-summer delight with a rich mountain laurel understory and the *East Loop* is a chance to experience a mature oak-hickory forest, decades in development ahead of its

Calvert
Phone Number - None
Website - acltweb.org
Admission Fee - None
Directions - *For Gravatt Tract*: Go 4 miles south on MD 2/4 from the intersection of MD 231 in Prince Frederick; left on Parkers Creek Road, cross MD 765 and then turn right onto Scientists' Cliffs Road; drive .8 miles to the ACLT parking lot on the left. *For Double Oak Farm*: Go two miles east on Dares Beach Road from the light on MD 2/4 in Prince Frederick. Turn right onto Double Oak Road and drive one mile. Turn left onto the lane across from open field, past house to designated parking.

neighbors regenerating after centuries in cultivation. Each of the loops can be completed in under an hour.

Trail Sense: The trails are blazed and a trail map available.

Dog Friendliness

Dogs are welcome on park trails.

Traffic

No bicycles or motorized vehicles are allowed on these lightly used foot-paths, except the East Loop at the Gavatt Tract. Double Oak Farm is closed to hikers for turkey hunting season - except for Sundays - during April and May and white-tailed deer season periodically from October through early January.

The park's namesake chestnut tree has recently fallen victim to the fatal blight.

Canine Swimming

Woodland ponds and streams conspire to keep your dog cool and Parkers Creek is available for dedicated dog paddlers.

Trail Time

Several hours to a half-day.

25
Potomac State Forest – Backbone Mountain

The Park

At 3,360 feet above sea level Backbone Mountain, a long slab of rock in the Allegheny range, is the highest point in Maryland, the 32nd highest "highpoint" in the United States. When you reach the summit you and your dog will actually be standing on the point of Hoye-Crest, named for Captain Charles Hoye, a prominent chronicler of Maryland lore and founder of the Garrett County Historical Society.

Backbone Mountain is the Eastern Continental Divide - rain that falls on the eastern slope drains into the Atlantic Ocean via the Potomac River and water on the western side eventually finds it way to the Gulf of Mexico.

Garrett

Phone Number
- None

Website
- None

Admission Fee
- None

Directions
- From Oakland, Maryland go south on Route 219 and cross over the intersection of Route 50 at Red House to Silver Lake, West Virginia. Staying on Route 219, go one mile south to an old logging road and park along the road.

The Walks

The highest point in Maryland is less than two football fields from West Virginia and the easiest way to get to Hoye-Crest is to start across the state line in the Monongahela National Forest. You will use an old logging road to reach the ridge of Backbone Mountain; it is steep enough to get your dog panting but not so arduous you will need to pull over and rest. Once you reach the ridge it is a short ways to the high point. The trail on the ridge is more of a hiking trail and has some interesting features the short time you are on it.

Once your dog is through soaking in the experience of being on the roof of Maryland the way down is the same as the way up - a two-mile round trip. There are plenty more trails to explore across Backbone Mountain but there won't be any wayfinding aids at the trailhead.

Another high point in the forest is the rock outcropping near the intersection of Maryland Route 135 and Walnut Bottom Road which overlooks a portion of Potomac State Forest, Savage River State Forest and Crabtree Creek. Your dog can go off leash in Potomac State Forest.

Trail Sense: The route to Hoye-Crest is blazed by the letters H.P.

Dog Friendliness
Dogs are welcome at the top of Maryland.

Traffic
There always seems to be somebody on Backbone Mountain looking for Hoye-Crest - just about anyone can make the climb - but it is seldom a parade to the top.

Canine Swimming
There is no water on the canine hike to Hoye-Crest.

Trail Time
About an hour to tag the summit and return to Route 219.

26
Appalachian Trail

The Park

Visionaries began talking about a footpath that would follow the crest of the Appalachian Mountains nearly the length of the East Coast back in the early 1900s. Based on proposals from Massachusetts regional planner Benton MacKaye the dream began to become a reality in 1921. Over the next two decades the *Appalachian Trail* was constructed and marked by volunteer hiking clubs.

A continuous trail opened in 1937 but hurricanes and highway construction pried open frustrating gaps until 1951 when all sections were relocated. The Appalachian National Scenic Trail now follows more than 2,100 miles in the United States - and about as many in Canada to the Gaspe Peninsula where the Appalachians eventually march into the sea.

The Appalachian Mountains are the oldest in the world - once higher than the Rockies but worn down and rounded by eons of subtle erosion. Still, hiking the Appalachians is some of the most challenging you can do with your dog as most of the routes charge straight up and down the peaks rather than using switchbacks.

Washington/Frederick

Phone Number
- None

Website
- www.dnr.state.md.us/public-lands/at.html

Admission Fee
- None

Directions
- Access from Route 40 parking lot east of Greenbrier State Park or in various parks: Gathland State Park or Harpers Ferry National Historic Park.

The Walks

Maryland contains 40 miles of the *Appalachian Trail*, all but two of which travel along the crest of South Mountain. You could complete the state crossing in an energetic weekend with your dog, although most canine hikers opt for day hikes, either out-and-back jaunts or via car shuttle. Elevations range from 250 feet at the Potomac River to a less-than lofty 1,900 feet at High Rock.

Your dog will find some rocky patches along the way but nothing like the going in some neighboring states - Pennsylvania for instance, where "boots go to die." By contrast the trail on South Mountain is almost like taking your dog down a country lane with wide, dirt passages in many places.

With a series of parks and the parking lot on Route 40 taking the *Appalachian Trail* in chunks is an easy thing to do. Popular destinations include Annapolis Rocks, about one hour north of Route 40 and Washington Monument about 90 minutes to the south. Both provide long views across the surrounding valleys with only a modest purchase.

Trail Sense: You can purchase a detailed map from the Potomac Appalachian Trail Club or study one at the Route 40 lot. The *Appalachian Trail* is blazed in white and side trails are marked in blue.

Dogs make the trek to Annapolis Rock for this view of Greenbrier Lake.

Dog Friendliness

Dogs are permitted on the Appalachian Trail in Maryland.

Traffic

The *Appalachian Trail* is for foot traffic only. Thanks to easy access and relatively gentle grades the trail gets plenty of use - with only one trail and everyone heading for the same destinations this canine hike can turn into quite a parade on beautiful weekend days.

Canine Swimming

There is a spring at Annapolis Rocks but no swimming so bring plenty of drinking water on this canine hike.

Trail Time

A minimum of a couple hours on a day hike.

27
Wheaton Regional Park

The Park

Rhode Island-born Frank Wheaton was one of the few American military officers to attain the rank of major general without attending West Point. He was commissioned as a first lieutenant in the cavalry in 1855 and saw considerable action on the Indian frontier. During the Civil War he received several battlefield promotions and was entrusted with the command of the defense of Washington from Fort Stevens just down Georgia Avenue from the park. Five years later the sparsely populated countryside nearby took the general's name.

Montgomery

Phone Number
- (301) 680-5376

Website
- www.mc-mncppc.org/parks/facilities/regional_parks/wheaton/

Admission Fee
- None

Directions
- From Georgia Avenue (MD 97) go east onto Randolph Road. Parking for the Brookside Nature Center is on the right.

Almost any way you can think to get around a park can be found in Wheaton. Horesback riding, cycling, skating are all on tap here. A replica of an 1863 C.P. Huntington steam engine pulls a miniature train on a 10-minute tour of the park. There is even a treasured 1915 carousel built by the legendary Herschell Spillman Co. of North Tonawanda, New York. The carousel was operated on the National Mall in the District from the 1960s to 1980s before finding a home in the park.

The Walks

Wheaton Regional Park was not put together on a whim - wide, crushed-gravel trails lead to the five distinct areas of the park. There are four miles of these paths but you will want to start your dog on the natural surface trails at the Brookside Nature Center. These well-groomed paths are a pleasure for any dog and even the bridle paths in the system are not unduly torn asunder.

These trails are lorded over by one of the most impressive stands of tulip poplar trees in Maryland. The tulip poplar is the world's largest member of the magnolia family and is the biggest, tallest native broadleaf tree in America. Historic tulip trees have topped 200 feet and while these aren't that big they will get your dog's attention.

At the nature center make sure to take your dog on the brief - but highly informative - *Woodland Walk*. Don't forget to try the bird calls to see the quizzical look on your dog's face.

The Thomas Harper cabin was typical of post-Civil War housing in rural Maryland.

Trail Sense: Park maps and a detailed mapboard are available. The named trails aren't blazed but signposts (with distances) are located at the many trail junctions.

Dog Friendliness
Dogs are allowed on all trails.

Traffic
This is a popular park in a busy area; no bikes or cycles are permitted in the natural area.

Canine Swimming
Pine Lake is an attractive 5-acre lake with flat, unvegetated banks for your dog to take a swim when it isn't busy with fishermen. The pond gained notoriety when the ferocious (to other fish, not your dog) Northern snakehead fish was pulled from its waters.

Trail Time
There are a wide variety of trail options in Wheaton Regional Park that permit anything from short, snappy canine hikes to a full morning.

28
Greenwell State Park

The Park

During his childhood John Phillip Greenwell's mother died, leaving his disabled father to raise the family's six children. Greenwell grew up to become a succussful Washington-area commercial real estate investor and in 1941 purchased Rosedale Farm.

Greenwell accurately refurbished the farm to its Revolutionary War-era beginnings. The focal point of the property was the Rosedale Manor with its Victorian rose garden that sits majestically above the Patuxent River.

In 1971 he deeded the 167-acre farm to the State of Maryland for use as a public park, with one important stipulation - it was to be used especially by those with disabilities. The State purchased the adjoining Bond farm and has agressively pursued Greenwell's vision for a park accessible to all. The therapeutic riding program is widely praised, there are camps for the disabled and on-going plans to make all activities in the park fully accessible.

St. Mary's

Phone Number
- (301) 373-9775

Website
- http://www.dnr.state.md.us/publiclands/southern/greenwell.html

Admission Fee
- None, donations accepted

Directions
- Take Route 235 towards Hollywood. Turn on to MD 245 East (Sotterley Gate Road) and travel 2.5 miles. Make a right on to Steerhorn Neck Road. The park entrance is the second drive on the left.

The Walks

Take your pick of canine hikes on these old farm roads. There are ten miles of multi-use trails on nine named routes from multiple parking lots. Where the trails leave the farm roads for footpaths some of the going can get a bit tricky but for the most part your dog will enjoy easy going at Greenwell.

You'll be hiking with your dog through cultivated soybean fields and along forest edges. If your dog tires of the sunny croplands, duck onto an inviting forest trail. Several routes meander down to the wide Patuxent River. About half of the trail system is open to hunting but these routes are easily passed over if the season is active.

Trail Sense: A park map is available at the trailhead and the trail junctions are marked by signposts.

Dog Friendliness
Dogs are allowed on all park trails.

Traffic
Horses and mountain bikes are allowed on all trails except the *Orange Trail* and *River Trail* near Rosedale Manor.

Canine Swimming
There is a small beach area and canoe launch with access to the Patuxent River.

Trail Time
Up to a half day of canine hiking.

29
Cosca Regional Park

The Park

Around midnight on April 14, 1865 John Wilkes Booth stopped at the Surratt Tavern just north of here on Brandywine Road. He was retrieving rifles, field glasses and other supplies he had stored there before going to Ford's Theatre to assassinate President Lincoln two hours earlier. The tavern owner, Mary E. Surratt would later be convicted for her role in the plot against Lincoln and be the first woman executed by the federal government.

Booth continued his escape through this area - although his exact route is uncertain - and would spend six days in southern Maryland before crossing the Potomac where he was captured and killed in Virginia six days later.

The 700-acre Louise F. Cosca Regional Park would open a century later in 1967.

Prince George's

Phone Number
- (301) 868-1397

Website
- www.pgparks.com/places/
parks/cosca.html

Admission Fee
- None

Directions
- From the Capital Beltway
(I-495), take Exit 7A South
(Branch Avenue/MD 5)
towards Waldorf. Turn right
onto Woodward Road and left
onto Brandywine Road.
Make a right onto Thrift Road
to the park and nature
center on the right.

The Walks

The canine hiking in Cosca Regional Park centers around the Clearwater Nature Center, tucked into a vibrant forest. Three loop trails set out from the nature center parking lot that can be traveled in their entirety or combined for a canine hiking loop of over two miles. The highlight is a trip around the 11-acre Cosca Lake, whose banks are brush-free for most of the loop. The paths are wide, the hill climbs are gradual and the tall trees are shady - what's not to love for your dog.

Off the *Lake Trail* you can also pick up the green-blazed *Perimeter Trail*

that leads to the campground and around the developed areas of the park. This route will take more than an hour to complete.

Trail Sense: A trail map is available and the color-coded trails are well-blazed.

Dog Friendliness
Dogs are allowed on the park trails.
Traffic
The trails are open to horses and bikes but once you get beyond the nature center and the lake, chances are you'll be alone with your dog.
Canine Swimming
There is plenty of access to Cosca Lake.
Trail Time
Several hours are available.

30
Little Bennett Regional Park

The Park

In 1750, when Frederick was considered a big western American town. The Great Road, now MD 355, was constructed to ease the transport of tobacco to the port of Georgetown. Then Washington became the compromise choice as the nation's capital forty years later and this Colonial artery became even busier.

Grist mills opened along the Little Bennett Creek and in 1798 Jesse Hyatt built a sort of "super" mill that gound corn for local farmers and wheat for export. By 1804 the mill supported the town of Hyattstown with six houses.

Growth spurted in the Little Bennett Valley and by 1860 it was a thriving rural community. It was important enough to skirmish over a couple of times in the Civil War.

Montgomery
Phone Number - (301) 972-6581
Website - www.mc-mncppc.org/Parks/enterprise/park_facilities/little_bennett/bennett_trails.shtm
Admission Fee - None
Directions - From I-270 take Exit 18 and head north on Clarksburg Road, MD 121. Turn left on MD 355 and then right into the Campground Entrance. There is also trailhead parking on Clarksburg Road across MD 355.

The Baltimore & Ohio railroad was siphoning much of the freight traffic off the Great Road but it wasn't until the 1950s and the building of I-270 that the nutrient-poor rocky slopes finally quit supporting this rural community. In 1975 the valley became Little Bennett Regional Park, Montgomery County's largest expanse of unbroken woodland at 3,700 acres.

The Walks

There is a full menu of canine hiking at Little Bennett Regional Park - 23 miles worth. Most dog owners will want to concentrate on the south side of Hyattsville Road where horses and bikes are banned. A dozen short, twisting trails explore the hollows and ridges around Little Bennett Creek and its tributaries. You can easily get a couple hours of trail time on these mown meadow and forested trails. When you reach the *Mound Builder Trail*, look down and not up for the mounds - they are the work of harmless Allegheny ants.

Don't give up on the multi-use trails just to keep your dog out of the path of the occasional bike or horse. The roads are rockier, the hills are steeper, the paths can be muddier but you will miss an eclectic mix of natural and historic delights - the 1893 Kingsley School House, fra-

This swinging bridge will give your dog quite a rollicking entrance to the Kingsley School House.

grant pine groves, stands of towering tulip poplars, engaging streams...

Trail Sense: A good trail map is available, posted at information boards and in the park brochure. The trails aren't blazed but use signposts and you'll need that map to keep 23 named trails straight.

Dog Friendliness
Dogs are permitted on all these park trails and in the campground.
Traffic
This is a big park and when the campground is not crowded you can go a long time in solitude.
Canine Swimming
Little Bennett Creek pools into small swimming holes but the water in the park is mostly for splashing.
Trail Time
As much as a full day of canine hiking.

31

Rock Creek Park

The Park

Although technically a national park, Rock Creek Park is more like a city park administered by the National Park Service. How many other national parks boast of ballfields and 30 picnic sites? It was the Army Corps of Engineers that first proposed the creation of Rock Creek Park when they considered moving the White House out of the mosquito-infested lowlands of downtown Washington after the Civil War. In 1890 Congress carved 1,754 acres from the Rock Creek Valley to establish the park, mostly in Washington, but spilling over to Montgomery County.

Montgomery

Phone Number
- (202) 282-1063

Website
- www.nps.gov/rocr/

Admission Fee
- None

Directions
- Rock Creek Park abuts the western edge of 16th Street, MD 29, running north to south. The main road through the park, Beach Drive, can be picked up from the north on the East West Highway, Route 410.

The Walks

The Rock Creek Valley runs from Lake Needwood outside of Rockville down through the main park in Washington D.C. An asphalt Rock Creek Hiker-Biker Trail travels the 13.6 miles through the scenic valley.

In Rock Creek Park you'll find two main parallel hiking trails running the length of the park from north to south on either side of Rock Creek. The wiser choice for canine hikers is the *Valley Trail* (blue blazes) on the east side. In contrast with its twin, the *Western Ridge Trail* (green blazes), there are fewer picnic areas and less competition for the trail. Each is a rooty and rocky frolic up and down the slopes above Rock Creek, a superb canine swimming hole. Numerous spur trails and bridle paths connect the two major arteries that connect at the north and south to create a loop about ten miles long.

Trail Sense: The trails are well-marked and the park service map keeps you oriented to the creek.

Dog Friendliness
Dogs are welcome in Rock Creek Park.

Traffic
Rock Creek is a very busy park; Beach Drive is closed to vehicles on weekends for recreation.

Canine Swimming
Rock Creek is usually better for splashing than swimming but there are some good spots for dog paddling.

Trail Time
A full day is possible.

32
Savage River State Forest

The Park

On May 1, 1755, British General Edward Braddock led a 2,400-man expedition - George Washington and Daniel Boone among them - along an Indian trail through this area. Their mission was to reach Fort Duquesne at the forks of the Ohio in what is now Pittsburgh - 122 miles distant. To do so the men needed to hack the trail to a width of 12 feet to allow horse-drawn wagons hauling cannons to pass.

Progress was slow, averaging just two miles a day with the men scrounging for wild game and rattlesnake meat for sustenance. Braddock's men were within seven miles of Fort Duquense when they were ambushed by a raiding party and vanquished. The rough road they carved out of the wilderness eventually became the main route west for settlers crossing the Eastern Continental Divide to reach the Ohio Valley.

Today a small piece of the original road survives on Big Savage Mountain, in Maryland's largest public space - the 54,000+ acres of Savage River State Forest.

The Walks

The gem of the Savage River State Forest trail system is the *Big Savage Trail* that traipses 17 miles through upland forests and old farmsteads across the crest of Big Savage Mountain. This popular backpacking trail, nationally acclaimed for its beauty and challenge, suffered damage from ice storms in 2002 but is back open to test your dog.

If you don't have a car shuttle or overnight backpacking gear for the Big Savage Trail there are day hikes on Meadow Mountain and Negro Mountain in the western sections of the park. The Negro Mountain system is an 8-mile horseshoe with steep slopes and stream crossings and Meadow Mountain features rocky canine hiking along its crest.

Trail Sense: Trail maps are available for these linear canine hikes.

Dog Friendliness
Dogs are welcome in all areas of the Savage River State Forest, including campgrounds but are not permitted in New Germany State Park that is part of the state forest.

Traffic
You can count on escaping with your dog on these trails.

Canine Swimming
Come to hike with your dog - this is not a canine swimmer's paradise.

Trail Time
Several hours to a full weekend.

"They are superior to human beings as companions.
They do not quarrel or argue with you.
They never talk about themselves but listen to you while you
talk about yourself, and keep an appearance of being interested
in the conversation."
-Jerome K. Jerome

33
Loch Raven Reservoir

The Park

Robert Gilmor, son of a successful Baltimore merchant, bought 2,000 acres in the Gunpowder River valley with dreams of building a castle resembling those of his ancestral Scotland. His mansion Glen Ellen never quite accomplished his vision and the estate was sold to the city just before he died in 1883. A dam and water tunnel to funnel water into Baltimore were built in 1881 and enough property was acquired by the 1920s to raise the height of the dam and create the 10-mile long Loch Raven Reservoir - the name being a tip of the hat to Robert Gilmor's beloved Scottish lochs.

Baltimore

Phone Number
- (410) 795-6151

Website
- None

Admission Fee
- None

Directions
- Loch Raven Reservoir is accessed from Exit 27 of the Baltimore Beltway (I-695) on Dulaney Valley Road (MD 146). Some of the more popular parking areas can be found on Seminary Road, Providence Road, Morgan Mill Road at Loch Raven Road, the Dulaney Valley Road bridge, Warren Road and at the end of Pot Springs Road.

The Walks

There is enough hiking on wide fire roads at Loch Raven to require days to complete. Throw in the ubiquitous side trails and it could take a dog's life to see the entire watershed. All the trails through the buffer zone around the "loch" are heavily wooded with mature trees that help protect the reservoir's water quality. Many of the trails track along high ridges with commanding views of the water, especially when the trees are not in leaf.

A day of hiking Loch Raven with your dog will involve many hill climbs, some that will leave both human and dog panting. There are stream crossings and rough stretches of trail, especially through ravines.

Trail Sense: Mapboards showing mountain biking routes are at some trailheads but for the most part you will be your own navigator. Orient yourself to the reservoir as you create hiking loops.

Dog Friendliness

Dogs are allowed on the trails throughout Loch Raven.

Traffic

Loch Raven is a hotbed for mountain bikers and you can encounter the occasional horse. Loch Raven Road is closed to traffic on the weekends from 10 a.m. to 5 p.m. to better accommodate recreational users. Trail use lessens north of Dulaney Valley Road.

Canine Swimming

Swimming and wading are not permitted in Loch Raven.

Trail Time

Up to a half-day around the water.

"Dog. A kind of additional or subsidiary Deity
designed to catch the overflow and surplus of the world's worship."
-Ambrose Bierce

34
Antietam
National Battlefield

The Park

On September 17, 1862, Robert E. Lee's first attempt to invade the North came to a climax. After his smashing victory at the First Battle of Bull Run in August, Lee marched his army of 41,000 Southerners against George McClellan's 87,000-man Army of the Potomac.

When silence fell again across the field, it had become "The Bloodiest Day" of the Civil War." Federal losses were 12,410, Confederate losses 10,700. The fighting was indecisive, but Lee's initial foray into the North was over.

Washington

Phone Number
- (301) 432-5124

Website
- www.nps.gov/anti/

Admission Fee
- Yes, a family entrance fee for three days

Directions
- From I-70 exit onto MD 65 South (Exit 29/29A). Go ten miles to the Visitor Center.

Great Britain now hesitated to recognize the new Confederate government and President Abraham Lincoln had the opportunity he needed to issue the Emancipation Proclamation, freeing all slaves in the states in rebellion.

The Walks

The 8.5-mile interpretive driving tour of the battlefield is one-way so it is really too far to do on foot with your dog but there are plenty of places to park and get out to explore, including the solemn "Bloody Lane" - an old sunken road separating area farms where the dead and wounded piled two to five feet deep in the dirt.

One place that demands to be explored on foot is the Burnside Bridge, southeast of Sharpsburg. Union General Ambrose Burnside and his 12,000-man force attempted to cross this 125-foot span over Antietam Creek at 9:30 a.m. on the morning of the battle but were held off by 450 Confederate sharpshooters hidden in the bluffs on the other side of the creek. The federals were not able to cross the bridge until early afternoon. At the Burnside Bridge you can access the *Snavely Ford Trail*, a 2.5-mile footpath that traces the creek around open fields. In addition to being a pleasant canine hiking loop, the trail conveys the agrarian feel of the area when two armies clashed here.

Trail Sense: Everything at the battlefield is laid out for you to follow.

Dog Friendliness
Dogs are welcome to visit Antietam National Battlefield.
Traffic
The Snavely Ford Trail is foot traffic only and seldom crowded.
Canine Swimming
There is some relief for dogs in Antietam Creek on a hot day.
Trail Time
Several hours.

Confederate cannon on the field at Antietam.

35
Cromwell Valley Park

The Park

Cromwell Valley Park is the result of the melding of three former farm properties by Baltimore County in 1994. The land has been cultivated for nearly 300 years and a Christmas tree farm still operates here. Four iron mines once produced ore near the headwaters of Minebank Run and the valley evolved into a major producer of agricultural lime. The remains of kilns used to cook Cockeysville marble into lime powder are still visible in a hillside along the stream.

Baltimore

Phone Number
- (410) 887-2503

Website
- www.co.ba.md.us/p.cfm/
agencies/recparks/cromwell.
cfm

Admission Fee
- None

Directions
- Cromwell Valley Park is east of Towson on Cromwell Bridge Road (MD 567), north of Exit 29 of the Baltimore Beltway (I-695).

The Walks

Still a young park, Cromwell Valley has already become a favorite with Baltimore area dog walkers. The park's 367 acres begin in a mile-wide riparian stream valley and taper across open fields and pastures until reaching upland forests.

Six short marked trails, totalling about 4 miles, visit all corners of Cromwell Valley. Most of the walking is on wide former farm roads. For a flat, easy stroll walk the length of the out-and-back *Minebank Run Trail* for 1.2 miles. Although you are only yards from the stream the water is seldom seen but the shrubs and small trees that shelter the banks are a haven for songbirds. The *Willow Grove Trail* climbs steadily to the top of a ridge for a loop through woods filled with tall, straight yellow poplar trees.

Trail Sense: A trail map is available at the parking lot. The trails are blazed but not always reliably so. This is generally not a concern except on the red-blazed Willow Grove Trail where a missed turn (easy to do) can land you on the Loch Raven trail system with its miles of uncharted hiking.

Dog Friendliness
Dogs are allowed throughout Cromwell Valley Park.
Traffic
Bikes and horses are not permitted on the park trails.
Canine Swimming
Minebank Run is a gurgling little flow of water that is good for cooling off on a hot day but little more.
Trail Time
More than an hour.

36
Piney Run Park

The Park

In 1975 Piney Run was dammed to provide drinking water for Sykesville. The resulting reservoir covers 298 acres and the surrounding park that grew up around the lake is another 200 acres.

The Walks

Piney Run Park features more than 5 miles of wooded lakeside trails. The marquee trail here is the 3.5-mile *Inlet Trail* but canine hikers may want to start explorations on the .7-mile *Field Trail Loop*, especially for early arrivers. Dogs are allowed on this trail off-leash and under voice control until 8:00 a.m. Despite its name, most of this trail is under groves of Norway Spruce, Scotch Pine and White Pine. The Field Trail also has the best access to the Piney Run shoreline of any of its four trails.

The Inlet Trail is essentially a long lasso of a trail with three scenic paths intersecting the loop. A surprising amount of this hike is on paw-friendly grass and the trails are uniformly wide and easy to walk. The Inlet Trail takes in both cultivated farm fields and a variety of forest habitats. Near the trailhead the Inlet Trail connects to the *Indian Trail* loop and then the *Lake Trail*, both wooded paths less than 1/2 mile long. The Lake Trail is a flat, semi-arc trail that features snatches of pretty lakeviews through the trees; the Indian Trail is a narrower pick-your-way hike in the deciduous forest.

Carroll

Phone Number
- (410) 795-3274

Website
- None

Admission Fee
- $4 for Carroll County residents; $5 for non-residents

Directions
- Piney Run Park is north of Sykesville. From Exit 76 of I-70 take MD 97 North. After 5 miles look for Obrecht Road and make a right. Go 1 mile and make a left on White Rock Road. After another mile make a right on Martz Road and follow to park at end. To reach the equestrian trails, stay on White Rock Road to Liberty Road (MD 26). Make a right and another right on Martz Road and go 1 mile to parking area.

Across the lake are nearly 4 miles of equestrian trails for hikers who prefer their trails a bit less groomed, but free of charge. The southern trail is a linear trail along the shoreline; the northern section features more loops. Again, these Piney Run trails are wooded.

Trail Sense: A trail map is available; signs indicate trailheads and wooden posts with inlaid painted circles mark the trails. If that isn't enough to keep you on course there are map signs scattered through the park.

Dog Friendliness
Dogs are permitted on the trails at Piney Run and you can picnic with the dog here as well.

Traffic
Bikes are allowed only on the Inlet Trail. Most of the people who pay to get in are more interested in the water activities than the hiking trails.

Canine Swimming
The trails seldom touch Piney Run Lake but when they do the dog paddling is excellent.

Trail Time
Several hours.

"We are alone, absolutely alone on this chance planet; and, amid all the forms of life that surround us, not one, excepting the dog, has made an alliance with us."
-Maurice Maeterlinck

37
Patuxent Research Refuge – North Tract

The Park

A scrawl of the pen by Franklin Roosevelt in 1936 established the Patuxent Research Refuge as America's only refuge to support wildlife research. The original 2,670 acres swelled to its current size of 12,750 acres with the addition of 8,100 acres formerly belonging to adjacent Fort Meade (visitors must sign a waiver regarding possible live ammunition encountered on the grounds - don't let your dog dig in strange holes!). It is said that the Patuxent Research Refuge is the largest patch of undeveloped green space that can be seen from the air on the east coast between Boston and Raleigh. There are two sections of the refuge open to the public: the National Wildlife in Prince Georges County and the North Tract.

Anne Arundel

Phone Number
- (301) 497-5580

Website
- patuxent.fws.gov

Admission Fee
- None

Directions
- The North Tract can be reached from the Baltimore-Washington Parkway, exiting to the east on Savage Road (MD 32). Make a right on Fort Meade Road (MD198) and after .7 miles a left on Bald Eagle Drive (marked by refuge sign).

The Walks

There are some 20 miles of trails in the North Tract, including the paved 8-mile Wildlife Loop access road which is lightly traveled. Another 9 miles of trails are on former access roads closed to vehicular traffic. The hiking on these pebbly roads cuts through the woods and, while quiet and solitary, the scenery seldom changes on the long, straight stretches.

The best hiking at the North Tract is on the *Forest Habitat Trail*, opposite the visitor center. The wide, soft trail contours pleasantly as it circles for 2.5 miles through mature forest with limited understory. Two other hiker-only trails of less then a mile are available: the *Little Patuxent River Trail* which loops through the moist ground by the river and the sandy *Pine Trail*.

Trail Sense: A descriptive trail map is available and the trails are marked at junctions with colored metal emblems.

Dog Friendliness

Dogs are permitted on all trails in the refuge.

Traffic

Will be light wherever you hike. Bikes and horses are restricted to the road-trails.

Canine Swimming

Several alluring ponds await canine swimmers including Rieve's Pond off the Blue Trail and the Cattail Pond at Bailey's Bridge. The Little Patuxent River a few feet from the pond has a deep pool at this point as well.

Trail Time

More than one hour.

38
Greenbelt Park

The Park

The story of Greenbelt Park is the tale of many a public park in Maryland - except this time the steward is the federal government.

This land was once covered with vibrant forests as far as the eye could see, all of which fell before the broadaxes of European colonists. For a century afterwards the ground poured forth sustenance for tobacco and corn until it could give no more. The land was abandoned and left barren.

As the land began to recover developers in the 1930s sketched plans to transform it into one of the many "model towns" slated to be developed around Washington D.C. As it happened, Greenbelt Park was acquired in 1950 along with the land to build the Baltmore-Washington Parkway and the recovering forest survived as an 1,100-acre oasis of passive greenspace.

Prince Georges

Phone Number
- (301) 344-4250

Website
- www.www.nps.gov/gree/

Admission Fee
- None

Directions
- FromI-95, take Exit 23 Kenilworth Avenue South to (Route 201) Greenbelt Road (Route 193). Make a left; the park is a quarter mile on the right.

The Walks

The first thing to know about canine hiking at Greenbelt Park is that parking is limited and visitors are encouraged to take advantage of public transportation so come early when you bring your dog. Once on the trails you will find well-groomed, wide paths - there are garbage cans out in the middle of the woods and the many tree blowdowns are attended to quickly.

Casual canine hikers can take advantage of the three nature loops, all around one mile in length. The *Azalea Trail* trips through streamlands to link the park's three picnic areas and the centrally-located *Dogwood Trail* highlights the regenerative forest with pioneering Virginia pines still able to steal a bit of light from the surrounding oaks and maples. Don't let your dog get discouraged

Bonus

Where can you visit Washington, D.C. and spend the night inside the Beltway with your dog for $14? Greenbelt Park. The park campground has 174 sites available on a first-come-first served basis and is open all year round.

A night in the Greenbelt campground is an inexpensive way to launch a visit to Washington with your dog.

at the stony dirt trail in the early going - soon enough she will trotting along on soft dirt and pine straw.

For a good long canine hike jump on the six-mile *Perimeter Trail*. If the droning traffic noise begins to intrude on your outing there are plenty of connector trails and roads to cut things short.

Trail Sense: The trailheads are well-marked, the trails are well-marked in colored blazes and you can grab a trailmap at the trailhead.

Dog Friendliness
Dogs are permitted on the trails and in the campground.

Traffic
Horses are allowed on the *Perimiter Trail* but they aren't available in the park so don't expect much equine competition for the trails. No bikes allowed on the natural trails.

Canine Swimming
Your dog can cool off in Deep Creek along the Perimeter Trail and in Still Creek but the water is not an attraction of the park.

Trail Time
A full afternoon to sample all the trails.

39
Eastern Neck
National Wildlife Refuge

The Park

When the glaciers of the last Ice Age thousands of years ago melted the rising waters swallowed enough land to create the Eastern Neck Island. The Woodland Period Indians settled here around 700 years ago, raising crops and harvesting shellfish.

European settlers arrived in the mid-1600s when Colonel Joseph Wickes and his partner, Thomas Hynson, were granted tracts until they owned all of Eastern Neck Island. Wickes built a mansion he called "Wickliffe" on the island that rivaled the finest homes of the era.

The Hynson heirs gradually sold all their holdings to the Wickes descendents by 1902. In 1950 land on Eastern Neck Island was sold to a developer who began planning a housing subdivision. Alarmed citizens appealed to the federal government and the U.S. Fish and Wildlife Service acquired the entire island between 1962 and 1967 to preserve its valuable wildlife habitat. The present refuge office is the only house ever built in the "Cape Chester" subdivision.

Kent

Phone Number
- (410) 639-7056

Website
- www.fws.gov/northeast/easternneck/

Admission Fee
- None

Directions
- From Route 301 take Route 213 North towards Chestertown. In Chestertown, turn onto MD 291 (also marked "to Rt. 20"). At the T-intersection, turn right onto MD 20 South towards Rock Hall. After 12 miles, at the blinking red light in Rock Hall, turn left onto MD 445 and continue six miles to the Refuge entrance bridge.

The Walks

There are several miles of quiet park roads that lead to different points on the island but you will want to concentrate on the short footpaths through the refuge. The shortest - but maybe not the quickest if you dally to admire the views - is the *Bayview-Butterfly Trail* that takes in expansive vistas on the Chesapeake Bay, a wooded pond and a restored grassland in less than one-half mile.

The *Duck Inn Trail* and *Boxes Point Trail* are out-and-back affairs that cover over a mile round-trip. The going is easy for your dog on wide, natural surfaces alternating between open fields and open forests. The trails lead to the wide Chester River with secluded sandy beaches and frisky waves that will excite any water-loving dog.

Trail Sense: The trailheads are well-marked and a park map helps you find them.

Dog Friendliness
Dogs are allowed on the refuge trails.
Traffic
Very light.
Canine Swimming
The open waters of the Chester River are accessed from the trails or at the boatramp at Bogles Wharf Landing.
Trail Time
More than one hour.

Small sandy beaches on the Chester River will be a highlight of your dog's visit to Eastern Neck NWR.

40
Elk Neck
State Park

The Park

In the summer of 1777 it was apparent that the British would launch an attack on Philadelphia from New York. But from which direction would the assault come? Would the British move overland through New Jersey or storm the colonial capital from the sea? In the end it would be neither.

In July the British set sail down the Atlantic Coast but scouts lost track of the armada. On August 24 at 4:00 AM Colonel Henry Hollingsworth, Deputy Quartermaster General, wrote an urgent letter to the Continental Congress in Philadelphia warning them of the arrival of the British Naval forces at Turkey Point on the Elk River.

Cecil

Phone Number
- (410) 287-5333

Website
- www.dnr.state.md.us/public-lands/central/elkneck.html

Admission Fee
- There is a day-use charge in season

Directions
- From I-95 exit onto Route 272 (North East Road)and go south 2.4 miles to Route 7 (East Cecil Avenue). Cross State Route 7, stay on Route 272 and go 11 miles to the end of the road and the park.

General Sir William Howe had sailed around the Delmarva peninsula and was landing unopposed. The next day more than 15,000 invading troops disembarked from 250 vessels to begin their march on Philadelphia from the south.

At Turkey Point the Northeast and Elk rivers have pinched a finger of land in the Upper Chesapeake Bay so violently that it swells to more than 100 feet above the water. The result is Elk Neck State Park, a vibrant mix of sandy beaches, marshlands and hardwood forests.

The Walks

There are five main trails at Elk Neck State Park. None is longer than two miles and all can be covered in a leisurely afternoon of canine hiking. The *White Trail* through the Thackery Swamp is a self-guiding nature trail. The *Black Trail* skirts the shoreline of the Elk River and the waters of the Chesapeake Bay can be reached from the *Blue Trail* at Turkey Point.

You start your explorations on an old access road high above the waters that soon turns towards the Old Turkey Point Lighthouse. The various footpaths radiate off the main trail across the peninsula.

Trail Sense: The trails are blazed and named by color. A map is available and the trails all connect to the main road.

Dog Friendliness
Dogs are allowed on the trails around Turkey Point and in the campgrounds but not on the North East Beach.

Traffic
The dirt parking lot is not large and on a pretty weekend day it will be filled. Most folks are just strolling to the lighthouse though so you can escape with your dog onto the foot trails.

Canine Swimming
The trails do lead down the cliffs to the Chesapeake Bay shoreline where you will find spirited dog swimming on small sandy beaches that are formed at gaps in the breakwater.

Trail Time
More than an hour.

There is no shortage of good sticks washed up on the shore at Elk Neck State Park.

41
Prettyboy Reservoir

The Park

In 1775 William Hoffman, recently arrived from Frankfurt, Germany, hacked his way through the wilderness to the West Branch of Great Gunpowder Falls to build Maryland's first paper mill. Hoffman's Clipper Mill is said to have produced paper for Continental currency during the Revolution. The state's paper industry thrived here for a century before giant mills in the West usurped its business. The river was dammed in 1933 to create Prettyboy Reservoir for a thirsty Baltimore. The colorful name survives from a local farmer's favorite horse that perished in a nearby stream.

Baltimore

Phone Number
- None

Website
- None

Admission Fee
- None

Directions
- Prettyboy Reservoir is southwest of Middletown, west of Exit 31 off I-83. Middletown Road will lead to several roads with trailheads including Spooks Hill Road, Beckleysville Road and Gunpowder Road.

The Walks

Baltimore City controls 7,380 heavily timbered acres along 46 miles of shoreline in the Prettyboy watershed. Hiking is almost exclusively on fire roads and involves many long climbs and descents. Ignore the occasional footpath that radiates off the grass-and-dirt roads - invariably they will lead to a dead-end or become overgrown.

Most of the trekking is done high above the water level and the reservoir is only rarely glimpsed. Instead, it is the richness of differing forest types and not lake views that is the enduring beauty of Prettyboy. The reservoir slopes have been regularly logged and the forests are in differing stages of succession.

Trail Sense: Fire road trailheads are marked by orange barrier posts. Beyond that there is nothing. The emergency fire roads will eventually collide with a main road.

Dog Friendliness
Dogs are permitted on the trails in the Prettyboy watershed.

Traffic
It is almost an event of cosmic intervention to encounter a horse, mountain biker or fellow hiker on the trail during an outing at lightly used Prettyboy Reservoir.

Canine Swimming
There is some splashing and dog paddling available in Gunpowder Falls but there are long stretches without water here.

Trail Time
More than one hour.

"The greatest pleasure of a dog is that you may make a fool of yourself with him, and not only will he not scold you, but will make a fool of himself too."
- Samuel Butler

42

Rocks State Park

The Park

The trails through dense forests along the Deer Creek are on the first Maryland lands purchased specifically to become a state park, back in 1951. The area was originally settled by the Susqehannock Indians who staged ceremonial gatherings at the massive 190-foot rock outcroppings known as the King and Queen Seat. Today Rocks State Park encompasses 900 acres of land in three separate parcels.

Harford

Phone Number
- (410) 557-7994

Website
- www.dnr.state.md.us/public-lands/central/rocks.html

Admission Fee
- There is a per person charge for use of the three picnic areas.

Directions
- The park office is in the Chrome Hill Road section, eight miles northwest of Bel Air on MD 24.

The Walks

Chrome Hill Road. The trails at the signature section of Rocks State Park all lead eventually to the top of King and Queen Seat. The views of the lush forestland from the top of the rock pile are spectacular but the outcroppings are unfenced and great care is required for dogs near the cliffs. These are challenging trails with severe climbs and narrow passages studded with rocks and exposed stumps in places. The *White Trail* is a sporty loop trail up and down and around the mountainous knob; it accounts for most of the four miles of trails at Chrome Hill Road. A low-lying *Nature Trail* loop is a short, pleasant walk opposite the Hills Grove Picnic Area on St. Clair Bridge Road.

Falling Branch. In this 67-acre sanctuary a path leads to the base of Kilgore Falls, Maryland's second-highest vertical waterfall. At the falls, trails cross the stream to the base and climb to the top of the 30-foot downspout.

Hidden Valley Natural Area. Quiet! That is what awaits you in this undeveloped tract of woods about five miles north of Rocks. Your one-mile stroll along level ground beside Deer Creek will end at an idyllic spot beneath a jagged rock crag protecting dark pines. While you drink in the serenity your dog will enjoy the spa-like rapids in the shallow stream.

Trail Sense: A trail map is available for Chrome Hill Road and the trails are well-marked with colored blazes. No map is needed in the other areas.

Dog Friendliness
Dogs are not permitted everywhere in Rocks State Park, like the three picnic areas.

Traffic
The postage stamp-sized parking lots capable of holding only a half-dozen or so cars are an immediate tip-off that your visit to Rocks will not involve a day of elbowing your way through the trails.

Canine Swimming
There is plenty of access to Deer Creek from the parking lots but not the trails. At Falling Branch you will find wonderful pockets of water ideal for a doggie dip.

Trail Time
Each section can be thoroughly explored in about an hour.

The entrance to the canine swimming hole at the base of Kilgore Falls.

43
St. Mary's City

The Park

In the early 1600s the English looked for ways to develop North America as quickly as possible. King Charles I granted what is now the state of Maryland to Cecil Calvert, the second Baron of Baltimore with the expectation that Calvert would trade land for settlement to his colonists and build trade with Mother England and profit to the Calvert family.

In November 1633 two ships, the *Ark* and the *Dove*, set sail under Governor Leonard Calvert's command and eventually sailed up the Potomac River. After discussions with the indigent tribes the newcomers put down along the St. Mary's River, using land already cleared by the Yaocomaco Indians, who were preparing to leave. St. Mary's was the fourth permanent English settlement in North America.

As more and more people took Lord Baltimore up on his offer of land the area's population grew and spread across the northern Potomac. In response, he chartered the town of St. Mary's in 1668. Community leaders were already meeting in Leonard Calvert's home and now Maryland had its first capital.

When Annapolis won the tussle for state capital in 1695 St. Mary's was simply abandoned. Nothing ever came to take its place, just nature and some agriculture. The remains of Maryland's first established colony settled under the dirt, waiting to be reidscovered by archaelogists.

St. Mary's
Phone Number - (800) 762-1634
Website - www.stmaryscity.org/
Admission Fee - Some exhibits charge fees seasonally
Directions - Historic St. Mary's City is located on MD 5.

The Walks

Your dog is welcome to explore St. Mary's City as it is resurrected - the outdoor museum is certainly one of the most attractive of active historical sites. Serpentine walking paths connect exhibits ranging from an Indian long-house to Maryland's first assembly house to a reconstructed chapel. The trail winds for three miles in open fields atop the wooded banks of the river and back to the former Splay Tobacco Plantation.

Trail Sense: There are mapboards to help interpret old St. Mary's City.

Dog Friendliness
Dogs are welcome to explore this outdoor museum.

Traffic
This is a quiet canine hike in the off-season but more communal on days of scheduled events.

Canine Swimming
Canine aquatics are not a part of this hike.

Trail Time
More than one hour.

Your dog can learn about Maryland's first capital in a scenic setting on the St. Mary's River.

44
Gunpowder Falls State Park-Jerusalem Mill

The Park

Established as a grain mill in 1772, Jerusalem Mill operated until 1961. Restoration began in 1985 and has expanded to include the entire Village of Jerusalem with tenant houses, smith shops, and a general store. Since 1995, the Jerusalem Mill has housed the administrative headquarters for all of sprawling Gunpowder Falls State Park.

Baltimore/Harford

Phone Number
- (410) 557-7994

Website
- www.dnr.statemd.uspublic-lands/central

Admission Fee
- None

Directions
- The park office is in Kingsville on Jerusalem Mill Road off US 1.

The Walks

There are many miles of hiking along the Little Gunpowder Falls on both sides of park headquarters here. Upstream from Jerusalem Mill the white-blazed *Little Gunpowder Trail* is a bouncing ramble through the woods. The return trip on the linear trail can loop into the hillsides on blue-blazed side trails like the *Quarry Trail*. **Caution:** This trail requires one crossing of the 4-lane US 1 and although the road is not heavily used at this point the southbound traffic does race downhill around a blind curve like a banked NASCAR track.

Downstream (cross the bridge by the Mill to pick up the trail) the route takes in more open fields as it leads to a loop around the Kingsville Athletic Fields. For a quick loop, stop at the Jericho Covered Bridge and return on the yellow-blazed horse trail.

Trail Sense: A trail map is available and the trails are well-marked.

Downstream from Jerusalem Mill about 1/2 mile is Jericho Covered Bridge, one of only six remaining covered bridges in Maryland and the only one of its kind in Baltimore and Harford counties.

Old folk wisdom held that these bridges were built to resemble a barn to entice a wary horse across water but the bridges are covered simply to protect the expensive wooden decks. The ford at this point across the Little Gunpowder Falls dates to Colonial times; the bridge was constructed in 1865.

Builder Thomas F. Forsyth used three truss types in its construction: the simple Multiple King Post; the horizontal Queen Post extension; and the Burr Arch, patented in 1804 by Theodore Burr, for stability. Renovated in 1981, the Jericho Covered Bridge still carries traffic.

Dog Friendliness
Dogs are permitted up and down the trails at Jerusalem Mills.

Traffic
The easy walking around Jerusalem Mill attracts many casual hikers and dog walkers; deep into the trails there is greater solitude.

Canine Swimming
The trails stay true to the whims of the Little Gunpowder Falls with many access points to the water.

Trail Time
Several hours to a full day.

"If there are no dogs in Heaven, then when I die I want to go where they went."
-Anonymous

45

Terrapin
Nature Park

The Park

The Terrapin Nature Park occupies almost one mile of Chesapeake Bay shoreline from the Chesapeake Bay Bridge northward. With its open dunesland, tidal ponds and oyster-shell paths this 276-acre park manages to exude a certain beach feel despite being hemmed in by its industrial neighbors.

The park is also the western terminus for the six-mile Cross Island Trail Park that spans Kent Island to the Kent Narrows.

The Walks

The stacked-loop trail system pushes through a combination of light woods and meadows towards the 4,000 feet of shoreline. The trail is sometimes gravel, sometimes oyster chaff and sometimes soft sand. There is a grassy shoulder if your dog finds the oyster shells uncomfortable under paw.

The paths twist for slightly over three miles and the going is easy over the flat terrain. Along the way are blinds to observe visiting waterfowl in the wetlands an an interpretive gazebo on the beach to gaze out on the open waters of the Chesapeake Bay.

If you are not looking for a complete crossing of Kent Island a good choice on the *Cross Island Trail* is old Love Point Park, a little more than one mile away. If you have a car shuttle there are several parking lots, including one at the Chesapeake Exploration Center that makes for a comfortable five-mile canine hike.

Trail Sense: There is a detailed mapboard at the parking lot to get you started in Terrapin Nature Park and a detailed trail map for *Cross Island Trail* Park.

Queen Anne's

Phone Number
- (410) 758-0835

Website
- www.discoverqueenannes.com

Admission Fee
- None

Directions
- Take Exit 37 - the first/last exit on the eastern shore - off US 50/301 and head north on MD 8. Turn left onto Skippack Parkway into the Chesapeake Bay Business Park and make a left on log Canoe Circle to the parking lot.

*With the fine swimming in Chesapeake Bay your dog can be excused if she
doesn't take time to admire the Bay Bridge.*

Dog Friendliness
Dogs are permitted on the trails and poop bags are provided.
Traffic
These trails are open to cyclists, hikers and runners.
Canine Swimming
If your dog shies away from the waves in the Chesapeake there is a cement
barrier that creates a calm-water pool.
Trail Time
From an hour, depending on how much time you spend on the beach, to a
half-day if you set out with your dog on the *Cross Island Trail*.

46
Cylburn Arboretum

The Park

Jesse Tyson, heir to a family chrome fortune, began developing Cylburn estate in 1863 by starting construction on a gray stone Second Empire mansion. His home was not ready to live in until 1888 and Tyson, a lifelong bachelor then in his 60s, celebrated by taking a 19-year old wife, Edyth Johns. "I have the fairest wife, the fastest horses and the finest house in Maryland," boasted Tyson. When he died 16 years later his wife carried on the family matrimonial tradition by marrying a younger man. When she died in 1942, husband Bruce Cotton sold the property to the city of Baltimore for a pittance so that the land would be used as a park. After housing neglected children for several years, the Cylburn Arboretum opened to the public in 1958.

Baltimore City

Phone Number
- (410) 396-0180

Website
- www.cylburnassociation.org/index.htm

Admission Fee
- None

Directions
- Cylburn Arboretum is in northwest Baltimore at 4915 Greenspring Lane.

The Walks

The 176 acres of Cylburn Arboretum's grounds are visited by five loop trails. These passageways are wide and paw-friendly soft dirt or cedar mulch but you will still want to stray off the paths to read the labels of the many ornamental trees. Most of the walking is easy going along the top of a wooded ridge although the *Woodland Trail* does plunge down a hillside. Beware of the *Witch-Hazel Trail* which is rocky under paw as it lopes down the same hill. There are also several garden areas to explore off the trails. The feature trail at Cylburn, the *Circle Trail*, is enveloped by the relentless pounding of traffic on I-83 but it eventually fades into white noise.

Trail Sense: A trail map and map of the grounds are available; large signs are posted at trail junctions.

The collection at Cylburn Arboretum features
several Maryland Big Tree Champions including an
Italian maple and a paperback maple.
Two easy champions to see are on the lawn in the right
front of the mansion: a *castor aralia* with large glossy
leaves and an Amur maackia.
Both trees are native to Asia and are resilient to pests.
The maackia is a member of the pea family discovered
by 19th century explorer Karlovich Maack along the
Amur River between Siberia and China.

Dog Friendliness
Unlike many nature centers, dogs are allowed at Cylburn Arboretum and
even welcome - the water fountain features a fill bowl for dogs.

Traffic
Only foot traffic is allowed on the *Wildflower Trails*.

Canine Swimming
Nope, none here.

Trail Time
More than one hour.

47
Hashawha Trails

The Park

Carroll County maintains nearly 8 acres of open space for every 100 residents and nearly 1900 of those acres are at the Union Mills Resorvoir Site. In 1972 the county purchased the land to establish the Bear Branch Nature Center and the surrounding Hashawha (an Indian term meaning "old fields") Environmental Center trails.

The Walks

There is something for every canine hiking taste at the well-designed Hashawha trails. Out for a simple trot? The blue blazed *Vista Trail* is a 1.2-mile circuit on mostly level ground that takes in fields, woods and ponds. Toss in the *Stream Trail* (green blazes) and you add a restored log cabin, grassy meadows, the gurgling Bear Branch Creek and a boardwalk crossing over part of Lake Hashawha. This blue-green circuit totals a bit less than 3 miles.

For longer hikes take to the wooded hills of the *Wilderness Trail* (yellow blazes) where four loops pile upon one another until reaching Big Pipe Creek. The complete outer loop brings 2.2 miles of rolling and sometimes rocky trails into your hiking day. Looking for an all-day hiking adventure? There are eight more miles of marked trails laid out by the Carroll County Equestrian Council, including the *Kowomu Trail*, beyond the Hashawha trails. These can also be accessed from their own parking lots; be aware that hunting restrictions close these trails from September through February on Mondays, Wednesdays and Fridays and for two weeks after Thanksgiving. Don't overlook the short interpretive *Bear Path Trail* behind the Nature Center that helps explain our everyday environment.

Carroll

Phone Number
- (410) 848-2517

Website
- ccgov.carr.org/hashawha

Admission Fee
- None

Directions
- Hashawha is north of Westminster. Go north on Route 97 and turn right on John Owings Road. Go 1.5 miles and make a left on Hashawha Road. The Nature Center is up the hill on the right.

Trail Sense: The trails are well-marked and trail maps and a mapboard are available at the Nature Center. Grab a map because there are many opportunities to slip mistakenly onto a crossing horse trail or adjoining private property.

Dog Friendliness
Dogs are permitted wherever you are allowed to hike.
Traffic
No horse or motorized vehicles are allowed on the Hashawha trails; the remote *Union Mills Equestrian Trails* may require yielding to the odd horse.
Canine Swimming
The streams at Hashawha provide a welcome splash on a hot day but aren't deep enough for extended dog paddling.
Trail Time
More than one hour.

"If your dog is fat, you aren't getting enough exercise."
- Anonymous

48
Blockhouse Point
Conservation Park

The Park

During the Civil War nine block-houses - small forts - were located on the Maryland side of the Potomac River between Great Falls and the Monocacy River. The blockhouse on this rocky outcropping overlooking the Chesapeake & Ohio Canal was built and guarded in 1862 by soldiers of the 19th Massachusetts Infantry. Off duty, soldiers clambered off the rocks and down to a camp built of logs, covered in dirt and shaped in the form of a Greek cross.

At the time of the Civil War, it was owned by William and Sarah Reading. Blockhouse Point remained in the Reading family until sold to Randell and Roselyn Patten in 1947. It was acquired by the Maryland-National Capitol Park and Planning Commission in 1970. Montgomery County began acquiring land from private area horse farms and has pieced together a 630-acre conservation area. There are no recreational amenities in the park.

The Walks

It doesn't seem like it when you pull into the parking lot but there is plenty of good climbing ahead for your dog here. Three more or less parallel trails dead-end at overlooks of the Chesapeake & Ohio Canal. The easiest way to forge a circuit hike out of the trio is to park at the smaller, unmarked western lot, but stop at the larger eastern lot to study the excellent trail map at the information board.

All the canine hiking here is under the canopy of a rich upland forest. Sprinkled in the understory are high-bush blueberry, spicebush, dogwood and even an active patch of paw-paw but most of the paths remain wide and clear.

Keep your dog close as you reach the point and pick your way down along the rocks for outstanding views of the Potomac River and the C&O Canal. You can access the canal towpath from the main parking lot for extended trail time with your dog.

Trail Sense: If you can't print a rudimentary map online, the map at the parking lot is a must-visit; the trails are not blazed.

Dog Friendliness
Dogs are permitted throughout Blockhouse Point.

Traffic
Bikes aren't allowed on these lightly used trails and horses are only permitted out near River Road.

Canine Swimming
There are streams in the ravines for splashing.

Trail Time
More than an hour.

Blockhouse Point overlooking the Potomac River is the endpoint for this canine hike.

49
Morgan Run Natural Envrionment Area

The Park

The land that would eventually be preserved as the Morgan Run Natural Environment Area was settled in the early 1700s when a stagecoach road (now Liberty Road) was established between Baltimore and Frederick. Carroll County leads Maryland in agricultural preservation and these 1,400 acres of natural land are slated to grow to more than 3,000 in the future.

The Walks

Step out of the car onto the gravel parking lot and this looks like a place to walk the dog. Wide grass trails cut into rolling fields dip and dart across the horizon into woodlands. There are many intersecting trails cut through the grass (sometimes high) to extend the canine hiking experience here. When the trails reach the wooded areas at the cold, clear waters of Morgan Run they continue to be a paw-friendly, hard-packed dirt.

There are unconnected trails on either side of Morgan Run in the flood-plain. Although these are hiker-only trails they are narrow and can be overgrown; a special trip to try them is not recommended.

Trail Sense: The trails are unmarked; trails maps exist but not at the park. Keep your internal gyroscope tuned up if you come without map and compass.

Carroll

Phone Number
- None

Website
- None

Admission Fee
- None

Directions
- Morgan Run NEA is south of Westminster, just off MD 97. After a left on Bartholow Road, turn left on Jim Bowers Road after .1 mile and another immediate left on Ben Rose Lane to the parking lot at the end in .6 mile. The hiking and angler trails are in the north section at the end of Jim Bowers Road off Nicodemus Road from MD 97.

> ## *Bonus*
> Hiking with the dog and the horse?
> Carroll County offers several equestrian trails
> but none with the feeling of vast open spaces
> like Morgan Run.

Dog Friendliness

Dogs are permitted on these trails; it seems a shame to come without one.

Traffic

These trails are popular with equestrians but not crowded. The routes along Morgan Run are hiker-only. Bikes are not allowed in this Designated Wildland Area either.

Canine Swimming

Morgan Run is a premier trout stream, especially in the winter. A modest five yards across in most places, it occasionally sports a canine swimming hole. A small pond can also sustain a doggie dip.

Trail Time

Several hours to an entire afternoon.

50
Quiet Waters Park

The Park

Traces of human habitation dating back 5000 years have been found along Harness Creek. The water's name descends from Englishman William Harness who claimed a tract of land here in 1652. For the next three centuries the original land was divided and sold into various estates until 1976 when the entire property was deeded to Mary Parker by the Simplicity Land Company. In 1987 Anne Arundel County purchased 336 acres of woodland on the banks of the South River and Harness Creek to create Quiet Waters Park, which opened in 1990.

Anne Arundel

Phone Number
- (410) 222-1777

Website
- web.aacpl.lib.md.us/
rp/parks/QuietWaters/

Admission Fee
- There is a $4 daily vehicle charge; closed on Tuesdays

Directions
- The park is located in south Annapolis on Quiet Waters Park Drive off Forest Drive.

The Walks

The dominant trail at Quiet Waters is an eliptical multi-use path that circles the many cultural and recreational amenities of the park from end to end. The east side of the path traverses grassy fields and wetlands while the west side is a curving exploration of the woodlands. There are so many contours that even on a crowded day you can find a bit of solitude on the trail. Several loops lead off the main 4-mile trail to views of the water. The walking is fairly easy and level throughout.

You may be tempted to step away from the wheeled traffic on this bike path and head down narrow dirt paths that radiate off the asphalt but do so only with an explorer's heart. The unmarked trails in the woods may or may not lead back to the main trail and may take you right off park property. Some of these natural trails roll up and down hills overlooking Harness Creek.

Trail Sense: A park map is available and will be very handy for hiking off the bike path.

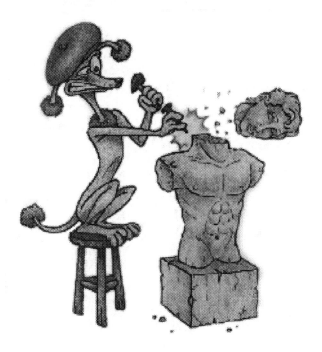

Dog Friendliness

Quiet Waters Park is home to Anne Arundel County's first off-leash dog park, covering an acre of the back of the park. There are two enclosures - a large romping area for active dogs and a smaller, shadier playground for smaller and older dogs.

Traffic

This is a popular and busy park.

Canine Swimming

Through the trees behind the dog park is a secluded stretch of South River beach just for swimming dogs. The waves are gentle enough to entice even the wariest dog into the water.

Trail Time

More than an hour.

51

Black Hill Regional Park

The Park

Open pit gold mining was conducted in this area for nearly a century between the 1850s and the 1950s. There was never enough precious metal discovered to trigger any gold rushes and when George Chadwick purchased land here for a summer retreat he converted the mine into a Cold War bomb shelter.

About a generation ago local water authorities looked over the privately owned farms and woods in this area and saw an emergency water-supply reservoir. Little Seneca Creek was dammed and the metro area's largest lake created. Black Hill Regional Park, a recreation park with 1,854 acres of rolling woodlands, picnic shelters, and water activities, opened in 1987.

Montgomery

Phone Number
- (301) 972-3476

Website
- www.mc-mncppc.org/parks/facilities/regional_parks/blackhill/index.shtm

Admission Fee
- None

Directions
- From I-270 take Exit 18 onto Clarksburg Road (MD 121) south. Turn left on West Old Baltimore Road to park entrance on the right. For the Ten Mile Creek Road area trails, turn right on Old Baltimore Road.

The Walks

The bulk of the canine hiking at Black Hill is around Lake Ridge Drive near the park office. The feature trail is the mostly-paved *Black Hill Trail* that loops a peninsula formed by two of the three major fingers of the Little Seneca Lake. There are plenty of access points to the trail here and if you are looking for a short day with your dog this is where you will need to park; trailhead parking for natural surface trails is limited to a lot at *Cabin Branch Trail* that will set you off on a long exploration of Cabin Branch and Little Seneca creeks.

Canine hikers may want to leave the main park to the picnickers and fishermen and head for the western area of the park across Clarksburg Road.

Here you'll find a trio of hiking loops leading away from Ten Mile Creek Road, an area of pretty streams and quiet woods. Off the old road trail the paths get hilly and your dog will earn his views of Little Seneca Lake.

Trail Sense: The trails are named but not blazed. The park trail map and signposts should keep you pointed in the right direction.

Dog Friendliness
Dogs are permitted on the trails at Black Hill Regional Park.
Traffic
Despite the many attractions in the park, the trails are relatively lightly used.
Canine Swimming
A good place to access Little Seneca Lake for your dog is the pull-off areas on Clarksburg Road and the *Hoyles Mill Trail*.
Trail Time
Several hours of canine hiking are available here.

Little Seneca Lake attracts swimmers of all types.

52
Truxtun Park

The Park

Truxtun Park remembers Thomas Truxtun, a privateer in the American Revolution who impressed George Washington enough to be brought into the new United States Navy. Truxtun, the 8th recipient of the Congressional Gold Medal, outfitted the *U.S.S. Constellation* and was the earliest known user of signal flags aboard ship in the American navy. Looking down on Spa Creek, Truxtun Park is the Maryland state capital's largest park, covering 70 acres.

Anne Arundel

Phone Number
- None

Website
- None

Admission Fee
- None

Directions
- The park is in Annapolis between Spa Road and Bay Ridge Avenue. The main entrance is on Primrose Road off Hilltop Lane.

The Walks

At Truxtun Park you'll be trading the sculptures, manicured grounds and forced walkways of nearby Quiet Waters Park for rusting hulks of abandoned autos and free-flowing, hard-packed dirt trails - which suits most dog owners just fine. The trails roll over two large wooded hills separated by a ravine. In the recreational part of the park the Annapolis Striders have constructed a crushed stone path with built-in steps to navigate the slopes and help arrest erosion. Natural trails, including one route on the ridge above Spa Creek, cross the more isolated back section of the park.

An extended canine hiking opportunity here is the *Spa Creek Trail*. This 1.5-mile route leaves Truxtun on a wooden bridge through high reeds and heads towards Spa Creek Conservancy and on to the former Bates High School.

Trail Sense: There are no maps and no trail guides. Get out and explore this compact park.

Dog Friendliness
Dogs are permitted across Truxtun Park.
Traffic
Truxtun can be a busy recreational park but the crowds seldom spill out onto the trails.
Canine Swimming
In a few spots the trails dip down to the waterline of Spa Creek for deep water canine aquatics.
Trail Time
About an hour.

53
Monocacy National Battlefield

The Park

On July 7, 1864, Union general Lew Wallace, better known as the author of *Ben Hur: A Tale of The Christ*, took up a defensive position with 2,700 men at Monocacy Junction, planning to check the advance of General Jubal Early and his 18,000 Confederates.

The bloody battle that came two days later was a decisive defeat for the outnumbered Federals, but the delay it caused Early probably kept Washington from falling into Confederate hands.

In 1847 a farm was cobbled together here from several small tracts that was purchased in 1862 by John Worthington. This farm saw withering action during the morning and mid-afternoon stages of the battle. In 1928, Glenn Worthington petitioned Congress to create a National Military Park at Monocacy. The bill passed but acquisition of land for preserving the battlefield did not take place for another half-century.

Frederick
Phone Number - (301) 662-3515
Website - www.nps.gov/mono/
Admission Fee - None
Directions - From I-70, take Exit 54 (Market Street), then turn south on MD 355. The Gambrill Mill Visitor Center is located one-tenth of a mile south of the Monocacy River bridge.

The Walks

Much of the battlefield is in private hands but there is still plenty to see in the farm land that is virtually unchanged since the Civil War. At the park Visitor Center an interpretive half-mile trail in light woods leads to the Monocacy River.

Down the road, a stacked loop explores the Worthington farm. There is a mix of open field canine hiking and hardwood forests on two stacked-loop trails. The park is devoted as much to the natural evolution of the landscape as to remembrance of battles fought. Of particular interest are the gnarly

Osage-orange trees that were grown as natural fences. The terrain grows steep in places but overall this is a relaxed hike for your dog on natural trails and graveled farm roads. All told there are more than three miles of trails at Worthington Farm.

Trail Sense: The trails are blazed and a map is availble for you to follow the events of July 9, 1864.

Dog Friendliness
Dogs are allowed on the park trails.
Traffic
Expect a quiet visit at Monocacy National Battlefield.
Canine Swimming
The Monocacy River is there for your dog to enjoy.
Trail Time
More than one hour.

"Happiness is dog-shaped."
-Chapman Pincher

54
Middle Patuxent Environmental Area

The Park

Charles Carroll, a devout Roman Catholic, left Ireland in 1688 to escape religious persecution and in 1702 acquired his first grant of 7,000 acres along the Middle Patuxent River. He would add another 3,000 acres and his son 50,000 more as the family grew to be the most powerful in Maryland. In the 1960s the Rouse Company deeded this property to Howard County when it was acquiring land to build nearby Columbia. Middle Patuxent Valley Association was organized in 1996 to protect 928 acres of diverse wildlife and vegetation in the Middle Patuxent Environmental Area, now managed by Howard County Parks and Recreation.

Howard
Phone Number - (410) 313-4726
Website - www.mpva.org/
Admission Fee - None
Directions - The park is located north of Clarksville. The entrance is on Trotter Road, east of Clarksville Road (MD 108).

The Walks

Although the going can get confusing at times, there are two basic hikes at Middle Patuxent. The main loop leading from the parking lot uses farm roads to reach the river and then circles back up to the crest of a ridge. Once you go down this trail you sign on for the entire loop which can take up to an hour. Often unmaintained, the hike can turn into a doggie steeplechase over fallen trees as the vegetation shifts from airy woodland to vibrant forest. Much of the trail is soft dirt but many areas are traversed on grass, a legacy of the Rouse days when the land was planted with ornamental olive trees and fescue grasses best suited for golf courses and lawns. If the grass has not been mowed it can be tough going. And watch for ticks!

The *Southwind Trail* has been created off the main loop and also leads to the river where majestic sycamore trees overhang the banks. The route travels up through Clegg's Meadow, decorated with warm-weather native grasses that have been reintroduced to the park.

Trail Sense: The *Southwind Trail* uses signposts but the main loop is sporadically marked. Consulting the map on the board in the parking lot is a must.

Dog Friendliness
Dogs are permitted on all the trails here.
Traffic
Foot traffic only is allowed at Middle Patuxent and it is light.
Canine Swimming
The banks of the Middle Patuxent River are often high but there is ample opportunity for a good swim.
Trail Time
More than an hour.

"And sometimes when you'd get up in the middle of the night you'd hear the reassuring thump, thump of her tail on the floor, letting you know that she was there and thinking of you."

-William Cole

55
Wye Island
NRMA

The Park

For more than 300 years Wye Island was privately owned and covered with tobacco and wheat fields. Farms passed in and out of the hands of a succession of interesting owners, including William Paca, third governor of Maryland and a signer of the Declaration of Independence.

In the 1770s Charles Beale Bordley left a prosperous law career to devote himself to farming and converting Wye Island into a private fiefdom. Under his stewardship the island became self-sufficient with its own vineyards, orchards, textile mills, brick foundry and brewery.

Over the decades the island fragmented under disparite ownership and in the mid-1970s the threat of encroaching development led the State of Maryland to purchase the island to ensure its future in a natural state.

Queen Anne's

Phone Number
- (410) 827-7577

Website
- www.dnr.state.md.us/public-lands/eastern/wyeisland.html

Admission Fee
- No

Directions
- From Route 50 turn south onto Carmichael Road. Travel 5.1 miles on Carmichael Road until you cross the Wye Island Bridge. From the Wye Island Bridge, travel south on Wye Island Road for approximately 4.2 miles. Numerous public parking areas are available along Wye Island Road.

The Walks

Wye Island featues about six miles of mostly multi-use trails that explore the tidal recesses betwen the Wye River and the Wye River East. Your dog will find paw-friendly grass and dirt paths - you trade the ease of these flat, low-lying trails for the mud in the winter.

Several of the trails are built around unique destinations. The *Holly Trail* leads to an American holly tree that was growing here before the Revolution. The *Ferry Landing Trail* was once the only access road to the island, lined with Osage Orange trees imported to serve as a natural fence. Osage orange trees originated in a small region of Texas, Oklahoma and Arkansas, which was home to the Osage Indians, who used its wood for bows. This mile-long path ends at a small, sandy beach. Another similar length canine hike is along the *Schoolhouse Woods Nature Trail* that rambles through one of the largest old-growth forests on the Eastern Shore.

The water trails at Wye Island are as attractive as the land ones. There are three soft landing sites that enable canoeists with dogs to stop and explore the land trails.

Trail Sense: Trail guides are available to navigate your way around Wye Island.

Dog Friendliness
Dogs are welcome across the island except at Duck House.
Traffic
Horses and bicycles are prohibited on the Schoolhouse Woods Nature Trail only.
Canine Swimming
There are plenty of opportunities for your dog to slip into the water for a doggie dip.
Trail Time
More than one hour.

56
Agricultural History Farm Park

The Park

The Agriculture History Farm exists to remind Marylanders of their agricultural heritage and to depict present-day farm life. Seventy acres of the 410-acre park have been set aside as a rural history musuem and other parts of the park have been created as demonstration gardens and fields.

The Walks

This is a sprawling countryside trail system that kicks off in big hills at the back of the park. Up the hill to the right will lead to the *Belgian Loop* around crop fields - don't spend time looking for a traditional band of trail as your dog will be bounding across open grass fields like a real farm dog.

In the other direction is the more traditional *Percheron Trail* that skips through the Pope Farm Nursery where trees, shrubs and ornamental plants are propigated for use across Montgomery County's 30,000 acres of parkland. The 1.4-mile natural surface path crosses Rock Creek and its tributaries several times before dead-ending in a neighborhood. A diverting 1.2-mile option is the wooded *Mule Skinner Loop* off the Percheron hike.

Trail Sense: A detailed map is posted on the information board at the parking lot and signposts lead the way out on the trails.

Montgomery

Phone Number
- (301) 495-2503

Website
- www.mc-mncppc.org/parks/facilities/ag_farm.shtm

Admission Fee
- No

Directions
- From Muncaster Mill Road (MD 115) take Muncaster Road north to the park entrance on the left.

Bonus
Montgomery County played an important role
in the Underground Railroad with many safe houses
established for escaping slaves traveling north to
freedom. Later Quaker communities helped establish
free black farms such as the cluster that existed here,
known as Newmantown. You can study the site that
contained three houses on 35 acres.

Dog Friendliness

Dogs are allowed to hike at the Agricultural History Farm.

Traffic

You may find more horses than hikers in this park.

Canine Swimming

There are creeks and farm ponds but this is not a dog paddler's park.

Trail Time

More than one hour.

The Agriculture History Farm is the place to bring your dog for a taste of traditional Maryland farm life.

57

Double Rock Park

The Park

The land that now contains the 102-acre Double Rock Park was part of a 3,000-acre tract first surveyed in 1735 for English overseers William Chetwynd and John Whitwick. It is believed the new owners were interested in exploiting the virgin forests that blanketed the hills they called Grin-don. Served only by a very narrow gravel toll road known as the Baltimore and Harford Turnpike, settlement came slowly to the area. In 1874, city surveyor Simon Jonas Martinet purchased 35 acres of land about one mile west of present-day Double Rock Park which he named Parkville. On the heels of the suburban migration following World War II, the park was dedicated in 1947.

Baltimore

Phone Number
- None

Website
- None

Admission Fee
- None

Directions
- From I-695 take Exit 31 South (Harford Road) to Parkville. After 1/4 mile cross Putty Hill Avenue at the top of a hill and go downhill for 1/2 mile to Texas Avenue. Turn left and go one mile to the end at Glen Road. Cross road into park entrance.

The Walks

A popular ball-playing and picnic park on the top of a hill, the active dog owner can find enchanting trails down below. The wide dirt paths are completely wooded with plenty of elevation changes throughout the trail system. The *Yellow Trail*, picked up to the right of the parking lot, works around the perimeter of the property and is joined at several junctions by the *Red Trail* which meanders down and around Stemmer's Run. The

Bonus

Save for the arboreal graffiti artist's assault on the many smooth-barked beeches on the hillsides, Double Rock offers a good imitation of a rural wilderness area. The immersion into nature happens quickly with a descent from the parking lot that immediately leaves the neighborhood houses behind. For a residential area the trails are clean (although the stream is a magnet for cups and bottles and wrappers).

stream was restored in 1997 and has a number of interesting nooks and crannies as it flows through the park. The blue-blazed *Falls Trail* starts down the stairs from the parking lot and follows a macadam path two-tenths of a mile to a small waterfall.

The namesake rocks for Double Rock Park mark the entrance and are not worth a special trip; more intriguing are the rock perches on the hillside above the stream that make ideal rest stops for a tired dog.

Trail Sense: There is no trail map available and no mapboard at the park. The blazes on the trails are easy to follow however.

Dog Friendliness
Dogs are permitted throughout Double Rock Park.

Traffic
The shady picnic pavilions get the bulk of the visitation; cross the stream and enjoy the less-traveled trails.

Canine Swimming
Stemmer's Run is not deep enough for anything other than a refreshing splash.

Trail Time
More than one hour.

"To err is human, to forgive, canine."
-Anonymous

58
Eden Mill
Nature Center

The Park

The first mill here was built in the early 1800s and named for Father Eden, a local priest. Save for a decade after World War I when the mill was converted into a power plant, flour, cornmeal and buckwheat were ground along Deer Creek almost continuously until 1964. At that point Harford County acquired the mill and surrounding 57 acres to settle the final owner's estate. The Eden Mill Nature Center was created in 1991 to preserve the mill and create the trail system through the property.

Harford

Phone Number
- (410) 836-3050

Website
- www.edenmill.org

Admission Fee
- None

Directions
- Eden Mill Park is seven miles west of Pylesville. The park is on Eden Mill Road off Fawn Grove Road between Route 136 (Harkins Road) and Route 165 (Federal Hill Road).

The Walks

There are 5 miles of trails at Eden Mill, including an elevated boardwalk, that stretch across 10 interconnecting paths. These trails are very easy on the paws - grass and soft dirt with only some rocky stretches on the incline of the *High Meadow Trail*. The *Bluebird Trail* is a special dog favorite with its grassy lanes through eye-high brush lending it the flavor of an English maze garden. The terrain at Eden Mill ranges from flat floodplain walking to hillside hiking that demand switchbacks to tackle the steep grades.

Trail Sense: A printed Trail Guide is available that allows you to create a hiking day of endless combinations of trails.

Dog Friendliness

Dogs are permitted on the trails at Eden Mill.

Traffic

No bikes, cycles, motor vehicles or horses are allowed on the trails - just walkers on two legs or four.

Canine Swimming

There is good access to Deer Creek, which generally flows lazily along at canal speed.

Trail Time

More than one hour.

59

Gunpowder Falls State Park–Pleasantville

The Park

This isolated trail system on the Little Gunpowder Falls comes to canine hikers courtesy of the Maryland and Pennsylvania Railroad, known affectionately as the Ma & Pa. To create the railbed nineteenth century railroad engineers clawed their way up the steep river valley here levelling hillsides and filling ravines. That railbed of the abandoned line now makes up the bulk of the hiking at Pleasantville.

The Walks

There are three hikes at Pleasantville, including a candidate for the "Least-Traveled Path" in the Baltimore area - the *Pleasantville Loop*. This 1.5-mile trek begins with one of the steepest climbs in the Gunpowder Falls State Park system to reach the start of the loop. Virtually indiscernible as a trail in most parts, let the dog lead the way and keep an eye out for white blazes. The loop follows a creative series of 270-degree turns through the thick forest with only occasional glimpses of the river below before returning to that steep stem trail.

The main hiking is across Pleasantville Road (a tricky crossing with a dog). Linear trails run along the river on both sides for two miles between Pleasantville and Bottom roads that can be combined for a loop across narrow bridges. The hike on the Baltimore County (white blazes) side is more topsy-turvy, tumbling in and out and around ravines; the Harford side (yellow blazes) uses more of the Ma & Pa trailbed, which crossed the river near the center of these trails, and is a bit tamer. It also adheres more closely to the flow of the river.

Baltimore/Harford

Phone Number
- (410) 557-7994

Website
- www.dnr.state.md. uspublic-lands/ central/gunpowder.html

Admission Fee
- No

Directions
- The Pleasantville section is southwest of Belair. From Harford Road (MD 147), take Fork Road west and make a right on either Bottom Road or, quickly following, Pleasantville Road. Parking is along the street and more plentiful at Bottom Road than Pleasantville.

The river is generally shallow enough to ford and shorten this 4-mile round trip.

Trail Sense: A trail map is available but not on site. The routes are always well-blazed in Gunpowder Falls State Park.

Dog Friendliness
Dogs are permitted on the trails at Pleasantville.
Traffic
These trails are so lightly used the lack of foot traffic can fail to keep the paths from getting overgrown.
Canine Swimming
Good, but there is not as much access to the river as might be expected due to high banks and vegetation.
Trail Time
Several hours.

*"Any man who does not like dogs and want them does not
deserve to be in the White House."*
-Calvin Coolidge

60
Rockburn Branch Park

The Park

In pre-Revolutionary times the Patapsco River was deep enough to welcome ocean-going ships as far upriver as this point, known as Elkridge Landing. Tobacco grown in Anne Arundel County fields (Howard County was formed in 1851) was housed and shipped here. The river was silting steadily, however, and the port was gone by 1800. Only the name plates of Landing Road in the 390-acre Rockburn Branch Park hints at the area's rich maritime heritage.

The Walks

There is plenty of dogwalking to be had in both the North and South areas of Rockburn Branch. The South area

Howard

Phone Number
- (410) 313-4955

Website
- www.co.ho.md.us/rprock.html

Admission Fee
- None

Directions
- There are two entrances to Rockburn Branch Park. The South area is on Montgomery Road off US Route 1 west and the North area is accessed from Landing Road off Montgomery Road.

features a 4.25-mile trail that slips through a wooded natural area. This amiable hike rolls up and down hills that represent the last gasp of the Piedmont plateau before it gives way to the coastal plain. Do not cross the power lines since the trails on the other side are part of Patapsco Valley State Park where dogs are not allowed.

The hiking in the North area is less formal, including lightly forested trails in and around the disc golf course. Also here is an open field walking loop and the former bridle paths of the Clover Hill plantation.

Trail Sense: A park map is posted on parking lot bulletin boards. The main trail is blazed in yellow and uses signposts at trail junctions.

Dog Friendliness

Dogs are permitted on the trails but not in the sports or picnic areas.

Traffic

This is a busy recreational park with activity on 8 athletic fields and picnic areas that spill onto the trails. Rockburn Branch is also a favorite with mountain bikers heading to the popular state park trails.

Canine Swimming

Rockburn Branch is a scenic, meandering little stream but not deep enough for canine aquatics. No ponds are in the park.

Trail Time

More than one hour.

"Money will buy a pretty good dog but it won't buy the wag of his tail."

-Josh Billings

61
Pocomoke River State Park

The Park

The Pocomoke River flows out of the Great Cypress Swamp in Delaware and moseys 45 miles across Maryland into the Cheaspeake Bay. The Pocomoke - from the Indian word for "black water" - has long been an important travel route and was believed to be an important link in the Underground Railroad where escaped slaves could hide in the swamp until nightfall when they could safely resume their journeys north.

The Pocomoke River State Forest and Park protects mre than 15,000 acres of woodlands more commonly seen in the Deep South - towering loblolly forests, eerie baldcypress swamps and great swaths of black gum trees.

Worcester

Phone Number
- (410) 632-2566

Website
- www.dnr.state.md.us/public-lands/eastern/pocomokeriver.html

Admission Fee
- None

Directions
- Take Route 13 south from Salisbury to the traffic light at Dividing Creek Road (Route 364). Turn left and stay on Route 364 to Milburn Landing entrance on the right.

The Walks

Pocomoke River State Park is divided into two sections about a half-hour's drive apart - you will want to take your dog to Milburn Landing since your best trail companion isn't permitted at Shad Landing. A trail using grassy fire roads and woodsy trails loops for 4.5 miles around the Pocomoke River Wildlands.

The star canine hike here is the leafy *Bald Cypress Nature Trail* that departs from the first parking lot at the Mattaponi Pavilion. To find the trailhead, turn right onto Mattaponi Road opposite the campground and make your first left. The trail is barely maintained in the early going and it takes awhile to reach the baldcypress swamp but there is extended walking along this unique natural treasure. All the walking in Pocomoke State Park is level and easy for any dog.

Trail Sense: The _Bald Cyrpess Nature Trail_ is unblazed but numbered signposts that corresponded to a trail guide long ago help keep you moving in the right direction. Look for the trail at a 45-degree angle to the right the first time you cross Mattaponi Road.

Dog Friendliness
Dogs are allowed at Milburn Landing but not at Shad Landing.
Traffic
These trails are generally lightly used; no bikes are permitted east of the Nassawango Road.
Canine Swimming
Pocomoke River is a fine place for your dog to swim.
Trail Time
Between one and two hours.

_The purpose of these baldcypress tree "knees" that extend out
from the man trees in the swamp is not fully understood,
but they make for an interesting trail._

62

Benjamin Banneker Historical Park

The Park

Molly Welsh, an English indentured servant, gained her freedom and began growing tobacco on this property around 1690. She soon bought two African slaves, freeing the one called "Banneky" and marrying him. Benjamin Banneker was the grandson of that union. He had gained a local reputation for mechanical and mathematical prowess when three Quaker brothers from Pennsylvania arrived in the 1770s to build a flour mill on the Patapsco River. The Ellicott brothers befriended Banneker and lent him books to fuel his isolated studies. In 1791 he left his one-room homestead for the only time in his life to help Andrew Ellicott survey the boundaries for the new capital city of Washington. Upon returning he published an annual almanac of his astronomical observations from 1792 to 1797. Thomas Jefferson lauded the self-taught farmer who is remembered as a pioneering African-American scientist. Baltimore County purchased Banneker's former property in 1985 to establish a museum and 142-acre park.

Baltimore

Phone Number
- (410) 887-1081

Website
- www.thefriendsofbanneker.org

Admission Fee
- No

Directions
- The park is just east of Ellicott City. The entrance is on Oella Avenue off Frederick Road (MD 144). Parking for the Trolley Trail is plentiful in a lot on Oella Aveue and at the western terminus of Edmundsen Avenue.

The Walks

Grand canine hiking lies behind an unpromising little mulched trail that leads into the woods behind the picnic area at the back of the musuem. The wood chip trail is a short loop through a forest thick with a spicebush understory. A wide trail then shoots off the back of the loop and rolls downhill into a stream valley that eventually leaves the park to join the *#9 Trolley Historic Trail*. Turn right and the paved path curves uphill towards a residential area thinly veiled

by border woods. To the left the trail slides downhill, following the Coopers
Branch until reaching an overlook of Ellicott City.

Trail Sense: No maps or trail markings are available. Ignore the tempting
side trails off the *Trolley Trail* - they lead uphill to deadends in backyards. A
rare exception is the short side path near the start of the boardwalk that leads
to a rock canyon carved by the tumbling Coopers Branch.

Dog Friendliness
Dogs are welcome in the park and on the #9 Trolley Trail.
Traffic
The #9 Trolley Trail is popular with dog walkers; fewer dogs take advantage
of the groomed dirt trail in Banneker Park.
Canine Swimming
Coopers Branch is good for a cool splash in rocky pools but not sustained
canine aquatics.
Trail Time
More than one hour.

63
Lake Waterford Park

The Park

This land was part of two land grants by Lord Baltimore, Gambriells Purchase and Howard's Pasture. An estate was carved from the property and a mill built to grind grain. After the mill was torn down in 1900 the area became known as a hiding place for hoboes. Subsequently, Waterford Mill, named for the 18th century Elizabeth Water, was farmed, used to raise commercial goldfish and even tried as a resort. Today Lake Waterford Park consists of 108 acres around the centerpiece 12-acre lake stocked with trout, carp, crappie, bass, pickerel and bluegill.

Anne Arundel

Phone Number
- (410) 222-6248

Website
- web.aacpl.lib.md.us/rp/ parks/lwp/index.html

Admission Fee
- None

Directions
- The park is in Pasadena at the corner of Pasadena Road and Waterford Road (MD 648).

The Walks

Don't dismiss Lake Waterford as another multi-use recreational trail upon seeing the paved paths at the trailheads. Beyond the picnic pavilions are a cornucopia of short, interconnecting nature trails. These are paw-friendly paths of sandy dirt and pine straw and the hiking is easy - wooden bridges and steps have been built to smooth out the rough spots.

The *Blue Trail* offers the most scenic diversion of the seven colored trails as it traces the lakeshore. There are many unmarked side trails as well, several of which are narrow fisherman's paths leading to the water. The trails are all wooded.

Trail Sense: A trail map is available but there is little chance of having to call out the St. Bernards here. The trails are not blazed but signposts lead the way at junction points.

Dog Friendliness
Dogs are permitted throughout Lake Waterford Park.
Traffic
Lake Waterford is a busy recreation and picnic park but competition is less fierce on the trails.
Canine Swimming
There are many access points along the trails for the dog to slip into Lake Waterford.
Trail Time
Less than one hour.

64
Northern Central Railroad Trail

The Park

The Northern Central Railroad began carrying passengers in 1838 but the road was known mostly to farmers and coal miners until November 18, 1863 when Abraham Lincoln boarded a regular coach, sitting with other passengers, headed for Gettysburg to dedicate a new national cemetery (contrary to popular folklore he did not scribble out the Gettysburg Address on the back of an envelope on the train). Less than two years later the President's funeral train would travel the same route. Passenger service would continue until 1972 when Hurricane Agnes finished the fading line by washing out bridges and tearing up track. The state of Maryland took possession of the NCRR in 1980 and after removing 600 tons of trash opened the first segment of the rail-trail in 1984.

Baltimore

Phone Number
- (410) 592-2897

Website
- www.dnr.state.md.us/
greenways/ncrt_trail.html

Admission Fee
- None

Directions
- The trail begins in Ashland, north of Cockeysville. From York Road (MD 45) turn right on Ashland Road. Stay on Ashland as main road bears left on Paper Mill Road and continue to parking lot at end.

The Walks

The 19.7-mile *Northern Central Railroad Trail* is the prettiest of the Baltimore area rail trails. Much of the route is decorated by isolated forests and meadows, occasionally dropping in on rustic farm towns. The first half of the trail roughly parallels the Big Gunpowder Falls (the Gunpowder Falls State Park administers the trail). The trail is broken up by nine parking lots so canine hikers with a two-car system can reduce the trail to manageable 2-3 mile segments. The crushed stone and clay path follows a gentle 1% grade to an imperceptible rise of 400 feet from south to north.

Trail Sense: Trail maps are available and posted in the parking areas. Wooden markers signal trail distances.

Dog Friendliness
Dogs are permitted on the Northern Central rail trail.

Traffic
There are plenty of bikes and pedestrians and even the occasional horse along the trail.

Canine Swimming
Opportunities for a a quick doggie dip are easier to come by along the southern stretches, and so is drinking water.

Trail Time
As much as a full day.

65
Fort Howard Park

The Park

The British selected North Point, now part of Fort Howard Park and the southernmost point in Baltimore County, as the landing site for a 6-ship invasion force on September 12, 1814. In the pre-dawn hours 4700 British marines disembarked here to begin a 17-mile march on Baltimore. Later that day the Americans engaged the force in the Battle of North Point, slowing the invaders and triggering a demoralizing chain of events for the British that hastened the end of the War of 1812. The army returned to North Point in 1899 to build Fort Howard as the headquarters for the coastal defense of Baltimore. The fort was named for John Edgar Howard of the Maryland Continental Army who received one of only 14 medals awarded during the American Revolution for his heroism at the Battle of Cowpens. In subsequent years the fort was an infantry training center (under General Douglas MacArthur for a time) through the Vietnam War, when a mock Vietnamese village was constructed here. The base was turned over to Baltimore County for use as a park in 1973.

Baltimore

Phone Number
- (410) 887-7529

Website
- None

Admission Fee
- None

Directions
- Follow North Point Road through Fort Howard to its end at the VA Hospital and make a left into the park.

The Walks

The *Endicott Trail* is a paved walk through the "Bulldog at Baltimore's Gate" that enables your dog to ramble through the gun batteries and ammunition magazines and to clamber on top of the earth-covered parapets that are camoflauged from the open water. Although a dummy grenade was found in the picnic area in 1988 it is unlikely your dog will sniff out any old ordnance here. A nature trail - bushwhacking may be required - leads to the marshy extremities of the shady 61-acre park. Another trail follows under a Ropes Course 20 feet up in the trees. Keep four feet on the ground here.

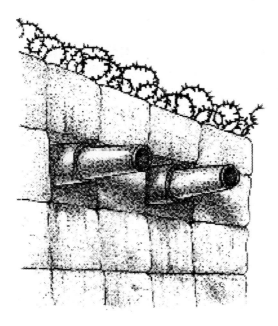

Trail Sense: There is a faded mapboard in the parking lot that will make more sense after you explore the park on your own.

Dog Friendliness
Dogs are permitted throughout Fort Howard Park.

Traffic
Fort Howard Park ambles on in comfortable anonymity under the nose of its more illustrious neighbor up the peninsula, North Point State Park.

Canine Swimming
The shoreline is mostly broken seawall but there is access to the open water at a small stone beach - beware of broken glass and shells on paws.

Trail Time
Less than one hour.

66
Chesapeake & Delaware Canal

The Park

Less than 20 years after the Delmarva Peninsula was settled by Europeans Augustine Herman, a Dutch envoy and mapmaker, observed that two great bodies of water, the Delaware River and Chesapeake Bay, were separated only by a narrow strip of land. Herman proposed that a waterway be built to connect the two - slicing 300 miles off the water route between Philadelphia and Baltimore.

It was a fine idea but no action was taken for almost 150 years. The first attempt to create a water link in 1804 was scuttled by a lack of money but the dream refused to die and by 1829 the Chesapeake & Delaware Canal was finally opened.

Cecil

Phone Number
- (410) 885-5622

Website
- www.nap.usace.army.mil/sb/c&d.htm#reach

Admission Fee
- None

Directions
- The western terminus of the canal is in Chesapeake City on MD 213.

The original canal featured locks but in 1906 President Theodore Roosevelt proposed the deepening of the canal into a sea-level, open waterway. Today the C&D Canal is one of only two commercially vital sea-level canals in the United States - and the only canal in the country built during the Golden Age of Canal Building of the 1820s serving its original purpose.

The Walks

The lands on either side of the Chesapeake and Delaware Canal are managed by the U.S. Army Corps of Engineers. Their mandate is to keep the maritime traffic flowing between Philadelphia and Baltimore, not to create a recreational paradise for you and your dog. Still, this can be an attractive place to bring your dog for some flat, easy canine hiking.

The full length of the canal is 14 miles so you will be not be going end-to-end and back, just as much as you want for your dog to experience the varied traffic on the canal from sea-going freighters to pleasure boaters to jet skiers. Your dog will be walking mostly on paw-friendly, packed sand roads that are occasionally paved. You can also find unmarked side trails along the canal.

Trail Sense: Straight out and straight back.

Dog Friendliness
Dogs are welcome along the Chesapeake & Delaware Canal.
Traffic
Expect to encounter the occasional cylist or even motorized vehicles.
Canine Swimming
The banks of the canal are well-fortified by rocks so the 40-foot deep waters are best left to boats.
Trail Time
Anywhere from a short stroll to a full day.

67
Leakin Park/
Gwynn Falls Park

The Park

In 1922 J. Wilson Leakin, an attorney of means, died and gave Baltimore money from his rental properties to buy a large city park. Planners settled on the Gwynns Falls valley in western Baltimore, once the boundary of the Iroquoian and Algonquian speaking tribes. Much of the original land for the park when it opened in 1948 came from the estate of Thomas Winens which overlooked the Dead Run valley. Today Leakin Park and the adjoining Gwynns Falls Park, at 686 acres the largest public park in Baltimore, comprise over 1000 acres of recreational opportunity.

Baltimore City

Phone Number
- (410) 557-7994

Website
- None

Admission Fee
- None

Directions
- The entrance to Leakin Park is on Windsor Mill Road; a centralized parking location for both parks and the Gwynns Falls Trail is at the Winans Meadow Trailhead on Franklintown Road.

The Walks

Gwynns Falls is largely undeveloped so most of your hiking will be in Leakin Park. The trails are surprisingly lush for an urban park, with a thick understory thriving beneath towering trees. The primeval feeling of the park is so pervasive it was chosen as a filming site for the horror film *Book of Shadows: Blair Witch 2.*

Hiking on the spider web of trails at Leakin Park can be rough going. Expect rocky surfaces under paw, overgrown trails at points, and hearty hill climbs (one trail descends 50 steps and doesn't even go halfway down the hill). Your reward is near complete immersion in nature just minutes from the bustle of America's 13th largest city. Remnants of the Winans estate are sprinkled throughout the park: the family home, an 1850s stone Victorian mansion called Crimea; a wedding chapel; a waterwheel; and ruins of a mock fort that may have been built during the Civil War to deter Union troops from attacking the Winans, who sided with the Confederate rebels.

The first 4.5 miles of a planned 14-mile trail to the Inner Harbor, *Gwynns Falls Trail*, has been completed to Leon Day Park. The highlight of the trail, which is part paved and part rocky dirt, is on the east side of Gwynns Falls where it uses the Mill Race Path, a filled-in mill race where Baltimoreans once strolled in the early part of the 20th century. The mill race remained level while Gwynns Falls dropped as far as 80 feet below.

Trail Sense: A color trail map is available and you will be consulting it constantly as you travel these trails which aren't blazed. Signs show the way along Gwynns Falls Trail.

Dog Friendliness
Dogs are permitted throughout Leakin/Gwynns Falls Park.
Traffic
These are very lightly used trails.
Canine Swimming
Dead Run is an aptly named trickle of a stream and access to the swift-flowing Gwynns Falls is limited.
Trail Time
More than one hour.

"My dog is worried about the economy because Alpo is up to 99 cents a can. That's almost $7.00 in dog money."
-Joe Weinstein

68
Liberty Reservoir

The Park

When Liberty Dam walled off the North Branch Patapsco River in 1953 a reservoir greater in size than Loch Raven and Prettyboy combined gurgled into being. Its 9200 slender acres contain 82 miles of shoreline. There are many miles of attractive, isolated hiking on fire roads in the Liberty watershed but access along busy roads can be problematic for dog owners. Also, skitterish dogs would do well to avoid Liberty Dam Road where you'll find the closest thing to a park on the reservoir. The police shooting range and a local gun club are located here.

Baltimore/Carroll

Phone Number
- None

Website
- None

Admission Fee
- None

Directions
- Liberty Reservoir is accessed primarily be three east-west roads that dissect the property: from north to south they are Westminster Road (MD 140), Deer Park Road, and Liberty Road (MD 26).

The Walks

The land in this valley before the plugging of the river was mostly pasture and cropland. Thus the wooded buffers around the reservoir are still filling in, giving these walks an airier feel than their water-holding cousins. But like Loch Raven and Prettyboy there is plenty of up-and-down hiking and the fire roads tend to make for long and straight routes.

There are several small creeks coursing through the watershed and trail crossings at these sites will be a wet shoe affair. Although not wide, officials have removed rocks from the stream bed to aide emergency vehicles in getting across. Good for trucks and dogs but not for hikers in cold weather.

Trail Sense: There is nothing. Come to Liberty with either a map drawn by someone who has hiked these trails or a very flexible schedule. The fire road trailheads are identified by orange barrier posts.

Dog Friendliness

Dogs are permitted in the Liberty Reservoir watershed.

Traffic

Some Liberty trails are open to bikes and horses but all trails are lightly used.

Canine Swimming

The tributary streams feeding into the reservoir are better for splashing than swimming.

Trail Time

Many hours.

69
North Point
State Park

The Park

When European settlers began cultivating the wetlands and fields here in the 1640s, they were the latest arrivals in a string of human inhabitants stretching back 9000 years. Notoriety came to the North Point area during the War of 1812 when local Free Staters engaged British invaders. Happier times arrived a century later with the establishment of a small amusement park known as Bay Shore Park. Bethlehem Steel purchased the land in the 1940s and tore down the park to establish a private hunting preserve for its executives. The public was invited back in 1989 after the State of Maryland acquired the property for conversion into a 1310-acre park with more than 6 miles of shoreline along the Chesapeake Bay, Back River and Shallow Creek.

Baltimore

Phone Number
- (410) 329-0757

Website
- www.dnr.state.md.us/
  publiclands/central/
  northpoint.html

Admission Fee
- Yes

Directions
- North Point is east of Edgemere. From I-695 east of Baltimore, take Exit 40 to Route 151 south; from the west, use Exit 43. Follow signs to Fort Howard on North Point Road (MD 20). The park entrance is on the left, 1/2 mile from Miller Island Road.

The Walks

More than half the park consists of the Black Marsh Wildlands, considered to be one of the finest examples of a tidal marsh on the Upper Chesapeake. Unfortunately your dog will not see this unique landscape - dogs are not permitted in the Wildlands.

You can hike around the short *Wetlands Trail Loop* which is a hard-packed dirt path. Also available is a hike/bike trail that skirts some of the fields at the park. The stone surface is not paw-friendly but does have wide grass shoulders. The old trolley line has been paved over in spots to form a nature trail. All the walking at North Point is flat and easy.

Although only 20 acres in size, the Bay Shore Park was considered one of the finest amusement parks ever built along the Chesapeake Bay.
Opened in 1906, the park featured an Edwardian-style dance hall, bowling alley and restaurant set in among gardens and curving pathways. There were rides such as a water toboggan and Sea Swing. Visitors would travel to the shore from Baltimore on a trolley line.
Most of the park was torn down after its closure in 1947 but you and the dog can explore the remains of a turn-of-the century amusement park including the wood-framed trolley station and the restored ornamental fountain. Complete your tour with a hike down the old Bayshore Pier that juts almost a quarter-mile into the wind-swept Bay - a diving board once operated where benches rest today.

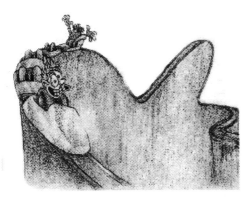

Trail Sense: A park map is available which indicates where trails are located.

Dog Friendliness

The opposite of most Maryland state parks, dogs are excluded from the wilderness areas and allowed in the developed parts of the park.

Traffic

Visitation is light enough to include the mile-long entrance road in your hiking agenda.

Canine Swimming

A small wading beach at the Visitor Center was opened in 1999 and dogs are welcome to dive in.

Trail Time

More than an hour.

70
BWI
Trail

The Park

The BWI Airport is the only commercial airport in the United States to offer visitors a recreational hiker/ biker trail. Portions of the trail, most of which sit on airport property, have been opening since 1994. The 12.5-mile trail encircles the airport and is patrolled by Anne Arundel County.

The Walks

This is quite likely the noisiest dog walk you will ever take - airplanes, car traffic, trains. But after awhile it all fades into white noise and becomes part of the experience of this unique trail. That said, there are pastoral refuges along the route including woodlands, pine groves and even a horse farm.

Anne Arundel

Phone Number
- (410) 222-6244

Website
- www.dnr.state.md.us/ greenways/bwi_trail.htm

Admission Fee
- None

Directions
- The BWI Trail is west of Glen Burnie and south of Linthicum. Trail access and parking can be found on Andover Road on the north side of the trail and Dorsey Road (MD 176) on the south.

For canine hikers the *BWI Trail* has several advantages over its rail-to-trail neighbors. Since it isn't constrained by a right-of-way, there is more grassy room on the shoulders for relief from the pounding of paw on asphalt (the trail is paved the entire way save for wooden boardwalks through wetlands); the trail was designed in a pleasing serpentine fashion; and there is a nice sprinkling of hills along the way. And, although few canine hikers are likely to care, the trail is a complete loop rather than an out-and-back.

No matter how you plan to use the BWI Trail, take along drinking water for your dog as it is scarce along the path.

Trail Sense: A trail map is available but not on site (use the Internet or local park offices sometimes have one). While you can't get lost, the map does give mileage between landmarks to help plan your canine hiking day.

Dog Friendliness
Dogs are permitted all along the trail.
Traffic
Although less crowded than the nearby Baltimore & Annapolis Trail, to which
the *BWI Trail* connects, there are still plenty of fast-moving humans in both
directions to look out for.
Canine Swimming
None
Trail Time
More than an hour.

71
Triadelphia
Recreation Area

The Park

Triadelphia was once a leading Maryland mill town with a bustling population of 400. Meaning "three brothers," for the trio of brothers-in-law who married Brooke sisters and built the original mills, Triadelphia was destroyed by the same 1889 rains that ignited the famous Johnstown flood in Pennsylvania. Already in decline before the deluge, the village was not rebuilt and it was a ghost town that was drowned under the reservoir that bears its name in 1942.

Howard/Montgomery

Phone Number
- None

Website
- None

Admission Fee
- None

Directions
- Triadelphia Reservoir is on the Montgomery County/Howard County border in the Patuxent River State Park. From Roxbury Mills Road (MD 97) cross the river and turn left on Triadelphia Lake Road to the parking lot.

The Walks

The Triadelphia Recreation Area was developed in the Patuxent Watershed for waterside picnicking and recreation. At the top of the boat launch steps lead to a linear trail that rises high above the reservoir and drops down along the Patuxent River to its terminus in a parking lot on MD 97. The route in Patuxent River State Park dips and rolls through the airy woods - few of the trees are old growth behemoths. The trail is narrow and easywalking as it skips along.

Trail Sense: No map is available but the trail is well-marked with red blazes (most helpfully placed at least seven feet high for easy spotting).

Dog Friendliness
Dogs are permitted on the trail along the Patuxent River.
Traffic
Not many adventurers stop for this pleasing linear trail.
Canine Swimming
The Patuxent River provides some of the best dog paddling in the Baltimore area with easy access from grassy banks to pools and spilling water.
Trail Time
Less than an hour.

72
Gillis Falls
Reservoir Site

The Park

Carroll County owns 1200 acres of land around the Middle Run and Gillis Falls where they are waiting approval to create a reservoir. In the meantime an equestrian trail system has been developed through the watershed by volunteers. These trails are closed Mondays, Wednesdays, Fridays and Saturdays from September 1 through February 28 and for two weeks beginning the Saturday after Thanksgiving due to a controlled hunting program.

The Walks

The Gillis Falls equestrian trails cover about 3.5 miles of wooded access roads. The terrain drops sharply in and out of the Gillis Falls stream valley on paths that feature many rocky stretches under paw. The elevation changes and varying moisture content of the soil conspire to allow differing forest types to dominate on different points of the hike. The trails are laid out in varying loops of short duration.

Hiking at Gillis Falls will necessitate at least two stream crossings and several more depending on your route. Only one bridge spans the sparkling clear stream waters. This is not a problem except at the confluence of Gillis Falls and Middle Branch which can be forded only by horse, dog or wet shoe.

Trail Sense: Trail maps are available but not at the trailhead. If you do not have a map, walk around the grass field in front of the parking lot and dip into the woods at obvious trail openings and begin exploring. Yellow and black-striped ribbons are unreliably placed on trees.

Carroll

Phone Number
- None

Website
- None

Admission Fee
- None

Directions
- The Gillis Falls equestrian trails are east of Mt. Airy. From I-70 take Woodbine Road (MD 94) north off Exit 73. Make a left in about 1 mile on Newport Road, following signs to Carroll County Equestrian Center on Grimville Road.

Dog Friendliness

Dogs are permitted on the Gillis Falls equestrian trails.

Traffic

Be on the lookout for an occasional horse on a cross-country outing but there is little competition for these trails.

Canine Swimming

Stream waters are seldom deep enough for canine aquatics beyond splashing.

Trail Time

More than one hour.

"If you pick up a starving dog and make him prosperous, he will not bite you; that is the principal difference between a dog and a man."
-Mark Twain

73
Fort McHenry
National Monument

The Park

Francis Scott Key was a 35-year old lawyer selected as an envoy to secure the release of American doctor William Beanes during the War of 1812. Sailing under a flag of truce, Key boarded the British flagship *Tonnant*. His mission was a success but Key was detained as the British bombardment of Fort McHenry, a star-shaped defender of Baltimore Harbor built in the late 1700s, began on the morning of September 13, 1814. After nearly two days of launching 1500 bombshells, the British abandoned their invasion.

Baltimore City
Phone Number - (410) 962-4290
Website - www.nps.gov/fomc/
Admission Fee - No
Directions - From I-95 take Exit 55 (Key Highway) to Lawrence Street. Turn left and left again on Fort Avenue to end.

Properly inspired, amateur poet Key scribbled out the lines to "The Defence of Fort McHenry" on the back of an envelope. It became the "Star-Spangled Banner" when performed by a Baltimore actor a month later and was adopted as America's national anthem on March 3, 1931. Two years later, Fort Mc Henry came under the direction of the National Park Service and today is the only area designated both a national moument and historic shrine.

The Walks

Fort McHenry rests on a 43-acre appendage of land in the mouth of Baltimore Harbor. There are large grassy open fields around the brick fort with plenty of room for romping for the dog. Cool breezes from the water and a grove of syacmore trees on the south side provide relief from the sun if needed. A concrete trail runs along all three sides of the seawall to create a loop of the park with plenty of opportunity to soak up historical monuments and shrines. A restored tidal wetland area keeps feeding and migratory birds arriving.

Trail Sense: None needed.

Dog Friendliness

Dogs are allowed everywhere at Fort McHenry except inside the fort itself but Francis Scott Key probably never set foot inside either (the National Park Service is unsure whether he did or not).

Traffic

This is a good place to socialize with other dogs, picnickers and kitefliers.

Canine Swimming

None.

Trail Time

Less than one hour.

74
Kinder Farm Park

The Park

In 1898 German immigrant A. Gustavus Kinder purchased 41 acres of farmland north of the Severn River and began growing fruits and vegetables for sale in Baltimore. The Kinders gradually expanded their agricultural operation until over 1,000 acres were under cultivation. After World War II, the Kinders moved from truck farming to cattle production and began selling off land for residential development. In 1979 they sold 288 acres of pastureland to Anne Arundel County for development as Kinder Farm Park.

Anne Arundel

Phone Number
- (410) 222-6115

Website
- web.aacpl.lib.md.us/
rp/parks/Kinder/

Admission Fee
- None; closed Tuesdays

Directions
- The park is in Millersville, just west of Governor Ritchie Highway (MD 2) on Jumpers Hole Road.

The Walks

A 2.4-mile asphalt trail snakes around the Kinder Farm property visiting fields and meadows and dipping into reforestation areas. This is easy walking and connects to the *East-West Boulevard Trail* for even longer excursions with your dog.

More interesting to the canine hiker are the unimproved farm roads that run through the park. These sand/dirt paths duck into woodlands and across old fields. For the dog who has never been to a farm, a trail leads past the farmhouse/park office (circa 1926) and a close-up view of four concrete silos.

Trail Sense: None of the trails are marked at Kinder Farm Park but a park map is available.

Bonus

Back beside the secluded Bunk's Pond is a forest
of bamboo, planted as an ornamental grass.
Although mostly associated with southeast Asia,
native bamboo is estimated to have once covered
5 million acres of the southeastern United States.
Many of the 1200 species of this hardy grass grow
eagerly in temperate regions like these timber bamboo
plants that have sprouted to over 25 feet tall.
They are wonderful at absorbing sound and
make this pondside walk a quiet, special place.
Beware under paw, however, as the trail has been
cut through the stalks.

Dog Friendliness

Dogs are permitted throughout Kinder Farm Park.

Traffic

The paved perimeter trail sees the most use; horses are permitted on the natural trails.

Canine Swimming

There are four small ponds at Kinder Farm but because of aquatic vegetation or limited access these are not prime doggie swimming holes.

Trail Time

More than one hour.

*"Ever consider what they must think of us?
I mean, here we come back from the grocery store
with the most amazing haul - chicken, pork,
half a cow...They must think we're the
greatest hunters on earth!"*

- Anne Tyler

75
Ma and Pa
Heritage Trail

The Park

The married couple in question are the states of Maryland and Pennsylvania which were wedded by a short-line railroad carrying freight and passengers between Baltimore and York. It took the peripatetic line 77.2 twisting miles of track to cover the 49-mile distance as the crow flies. The much beloved Ma and Pa operated from 1901 until 1956, hauling enough milk from area dairy farms to be known as the "Milky Way." The Foundation for the Preservation of the Ma and Pa Railroad set out in the mid-1990s to create a hiker/biker trail on seven miles of the old railroad bed in the Bel Air/Forest Hill area.

Harford

Phone Number
- (410) 638-3535

Website
- None

Admission Fee
- None

Directions
- Parking for Phase I is available at Tollgate Road opposite the Equestrian Center and on Mast Street, one block west of Route 924. To access Phase II, use Blake's Venture Park on Melrose Lane or Friends Park on Jarrettsville Road in Forest Hill.

The Walks

The *Ma and Pa Trail* is a stone dust path that differs from its other "rail-to-trail" brethren by its abundance of dips and swirls in the trail, a legacy of the local line's 476 curves. Much of the route is wooded although there is never a feeling of "getting away from it all" along the route. The tunnel under MD 24 was built especially for equestrians from a less congested age. There is also hiking available in 421-acre Heavenly Waters Park, although dogs are confined to a macadam trail aound the duck pond.

Trail Sense: A trail map is available for you to see where this linear trail will eventually take you. Mile markers are posted along the route.

Dog Friendliness

Dogs are allowed to chug along the *Ma and Pa Trail*.

Traffic

The Ma and Pa Heritage Corridor is a busy trail and you can count on many dogs, bikes, strollers and the occasional horse (in Phase 1 only).

Canine Swimming

There are no real dog dipping opportunities along the trail with only limited stream access available.

Trail Time

More than one hour.

"He is very imprudent, a dog is. He never makes it his business to inquire whether you are in the right or in the wrong, never bothers as to whether you are going up or down upon life's ladder, never asks whether you are rich or poor, silly or wise, sinner or saint.""

-Jerome K. Jerome

76
Chesapeake & Ohio Canal
Allegany County
From I-68 exit into downtown Cumberland, following signs for the Cumberland Visitor Center.

The Chesapeake & Ohio Canal, dubbed the "Great National Project" when launched by President John Quincy Adams in 1828, ended here, nearly 300 miles short of its goal of Pittsburgh, Pennsylvania. The canine hiking on the towpath at the western terminus in Cumberland provides glimpses into a history of American transportation that includes canals, railroads and the National Road. You will be atop the highest elevation on the C&O Canal at 605 feet but, like any stretch on the canal, this is easy going for your dog.

Aqueducts, like this one over the Monocacy River, were used to carry the canal across water. The Monocacy Aqueduct was so wonderfully constructed that two attempts by Confederate saboteurs and tons of flood debris over the years have failed to bring it down.

77
Flag Ponds Nature Park

Calvert County
Ten miles south of Prince Frederick on MD 4, turn left at sign.

Most visitors to this small Chesapeake Bay park will jump on the main half-mile trail to the sandy beach but canine hikers know better. The *North Ridge Trail* will lead to two freshwater woodland ponds in the course of a mile or so. The *North Loop* provides another half-mile of quiet canine hiking. As you go keep an eye out for the abundant Blue Flag Iris wildflower that gives the park its name.

When you finally decide to head down to the beach with your dog you will pass the relics of a major "pound net" fishery that operated here until 1955. One shanty that housed fishermen in season has survived to house an interpretive exhibit of the Bay's historic fishing industry.

78
Green Ridge State Forest

Allegany County
Eight miles east of Flintstone off I-68 at Exit 64.

Today Green Ridge State Forest is Maryland's second largest with over 40,000 tree-covered acres. A century ago your dog would have hiked long and far to find a tree here. Iron mining and sawmills depleted the forest and what trees were still surviving in the early 1900s were burned or cut by the Merten family who converted the forest into "the largest apple orchard in the universe." The orchard failed in 1918 and in 1931 the State of Maryland acquired the first acreage here and began the forest's renaissance.

Canine hiking in the state forest is concentrated along the *Green Ridge Hiking Trail*, a 24-mile linear trail that can be chopped into a handful of day hikes. Or launch a multi-day backpacking expedition - you can even tie in with the Chesapeake & Ohio Canal towpath for a circuit hike of almost 50 miles. If your dog loves water, he might be up for it - mountain streams and swimming holes abound along this trail.

79
Garrett State Forest

Garrett County
Five miles northwest of Oakland, off U.S. Route 219.

In 1906 Robert and John Garrett, descendents of Baltimore & Ohio railroad baron John Work Garrett, donated 1,917 acres for what became Maryland's first state forest. Today the forest covers more than 7,000 acres of wooded slopes and valleys. Mountain streams drip into swamps and bogs.

The state forest includes two state parks, one of which - Herrington Manor - doesn't allow dogs so canine hiking here is limited to old logging roads and the gravelly Snaggy Mountain Road. This is not difficult hiking for your dog with long, steady ascents and your dog can go off leash in Garrett State Forest.

80
Cabin John Regional Park

Montgomery County
South of Rockville between Tuckerman Road to the north and Democracy Boulevard to the south.

Cabin John Creek flows from Rockville down to the Potomac River. For much of its length it is now accompanied by a natural surface trail, partly maintained by the Potomac Appalachian Trail Club. Since the trail is in an urban area, dog owners must navigate across many busy roads in the course of its 8.8-miles.

The best way for canine hikers to experience the short, steep hills and wooded stream valley is in Cabin John Regional Park. Although the blue-blazed, out-and-back *Cabin John Trail* is the star of the park there are several side trips you can take with your dog to produce small loops and detours. Bikes can use the trails but not horses.

81
Rocky Gap State Park

Allegany County
Exit 50 off I-68 for Rocky Gap State Park.

The main canine hike here is the *Lakeside Loop* that travels for four miles around Lake Habeeb. In season this is a busy resort-type park and you will be taking your dog past a campground, a lodge, pavilions, a golf course, tennis courts...and all the people using the facilities.

There are stretches of memorable mountain scenery and, save for some rocky patches, relatively easy hiking for your dog. An alternate route leads to Evitts Mountain and the overgrown homesite of the original white settler who came to the area in the 1700s, supposedly to live out his life as a hermit after a disastrous love affair. History doesn't remember if he at least brought a dog with him.

82
Big Run State Park

Garrett County
From I-68 take Exit 22 and follow Chestnut Ridge Road south. Turn left onto Germany Road; park office is two miles on right and the trailhead is further down the road near campsite #3.

The Savage River Reservoir is the star at Big Run State Park but while most park visitors are heading for the boat launch canine hikers can enjoy the scenic *Monroe Run Trail*. Formerly a connection road built in the 1930s by the Civilian Conservation Corps, this 6.4-mile linear trail drops about 500 feet through an untouched stream valley. One thing you'll remember from this ramble are the frequent, unbridged stream crossings - you dog will need her toes on all four paws to count them all.

83
Naylor Mill Park

Wicomico County

Take US 13 and turn onto Naylor Mill Road north of Salisbury, heading west. The park is on the right after a mile in the Henry S. Parker Athletic Complex.

Salisbury gets some of its drinking water from the Paleo Channel Aquifer here, drawing water from between 160 and 195 feet below the earth's surface. The park is a cooperative of the water company, Maryland's Open Space Program and the citizens of Wicomico County. When you enter the park athletic fields will be on your right and the wooded trail system on your left. There are no signs but drive to back parking lot and enter the trails there.

Your dog will love the mixed sand and soft dirt surface of these paths that show a surprising amount of elevation change for the heart of the Eastern Shore. You'll actually be working along a ridge above swampy wetlands for awhile. The trails are narrow and tight, designed by the local mountain biking community that cut them. You'll find more than an hour of exploring at Naylor Mill Park, all under a mixed-forest canopy.

84
Watkins Regional Park

Prince George's County

From the Capital Beltway (I-495), take Exit 15A onto Central Avenue, heading east. After three miles turn right onto Watkins Park Drive (MD 193) to park.

This is a big recreational park with plenty to offer - in addition to the requisite athletic fields, playground and picnic shelters visitors can find a working farm, nature center, campground, classic carousel, miniature golf course and a miniature train. There is still room for your dog, however, on several miles of trails.

The *Spicebush Trail* circles the activity centers in its course of three miles. The *Beaver Pond* and *Overlook Trail* escape the hustle and bustle into the deciduous forest at the southern end of the park. These are out-and-back canine hikes with your highlight being a small woodland pond.

85
Seneca Creek State Park

Montgomery County

On Clopper Road North off Exit 10 of I-270. For dog owners, pass the park entrance, cross Germantown Road and take an immediate left on Schaeffer Road. Go two miles to the trailhead on the left.

The Seneca Valley possessed everything European settlers craved upon arriving in the late 1600s: rich soil for crops, more fish and game than could be hunted in a lifetime, and tumbling streams to power their mills. The plentiful red Seneca Sandstone was quarried for building, including the Chesapeake & Ohio Canal and the original Smithsonian Institution "Castle" on the National Mall.

Seneca Creek State Park preserves more than 6,000 acres of open space, including the beautiful area around Clopper Lake. Your dog, regrettably, will see little of it. Dogs are shuffled off to the Schaeffer Farm Trail System, 10 miles of dirt paths designed, built and maintained by local mountain bike clubs. And it shows. The trails all leave a single trailhead and the shortest loop is an easy 15-minute bike ride but one that will take 45 minutes by paw. There are no great destinations here - just hours of trail time with your dog.

86
Matapeake Park

Queen Anne's County

From US 50/301 in Stevensville exit to South MD 8 and turn right on Marine Academy Drive to park on the right.

This small park on the Chesapeake Bay features a pleasant one-mile wood-chip trail through a pine forest but the reason to come here is a stretch of sandy beach where your dog is welcome off-leash. The beach is a bit too industrial for sunbathers which makes it the perfect place for dogs to romp. Matapeake Park is just south of the Bay Bridge with splendid views of the bay and bridge. Dogs are not allowed in the fishing pier area of the park.

87
St. Mary's River State Park

St. Mary's County
Three miles north of Great Mills, off Route 5 on Camp Cosoma Road.

Come down near to southern Maryland is one of the longest walks around a lake you can take with your dog in the state. St. Mary's River State Park has two sections: one, a thickly wooded section that looks like it would be teeming with trails is actually undeveloped; the second, a 250-acre lake, is your destination.

The narrow trail follows the shoreline for 11.5 miles although you can cut the route by about three miles. The trail is used mostly by bikers and equestrians but is lightly used at any time. If you want to fill an afternoon with easy hiking with your dog beside a scenic lake, St. Mary's is for you. And don't come on a time constraint - the unmarked trails that bop off the main drag make it easy to find yourself on one you never intended to start down.

88
Furnacetown

Worcester County
Furnacetown is west of Snow Hill. Take US 50 East to Salisbury and pick up MD12 south. Make a right on Old Furnace Road to the complex on the left.

The brick stack of the Nassawango Furnace was constructed in 1832 to process bog ore, which wsa collected from the swampy soil along the Nassawango Creek. Maryland's only bog ore smelter flourished for two decades, supporting a bustling community of over 300 people. But as high grade iron ore deposits were discovered when Americans settled the Great Lakes region the need for this low-quality iron evaporated. The 19th century furnace and industrial village interpret this unique chapter in Maryland life.

Dogs are not allowed in Furnacetown or on its nature trail but the parking lot can be a jumping off point for explorations in the surrounding Pocomoke State Forest. You'll find some wide access roads and informal footpaths that support miles of flat, easy canine hiking.

89
Frederick Municipal Forest
Frederick County
Northwest of Frederick at the end of Gambrill State Park Road or at the end of Mountaindale Road off US 15.

Do you favor your hikes with your dog on groomed trails with a detailed map in your hand? If so, do not bother with Frederick Municipal Forest. There are no maps, no markings and no trail maintenance here (although you may catch the blue-blazed *Catoctin Trail* that is running 26 miles across the ridge). Bring your dog with a mind to explore for hours in the solitude of a mountain forest.

You will be traveling mostly on fire roads and expect to push your way across many blowdowns of big trees. The forest is managed to protect the watershed servicing the city of Frederick. You will stumble across many small ponds - these ponds gained national notoriety as a target in the national anthrax scare a few years back, but that isn't any reason to keep your dog from a good swim.

90
Rosaryville State Park
Prince George's County
Off US 301, just south of Osborne Road.

Charles Calvert, the Third Lord of Baltimore built a hunting lodge here in 1660 - a large 50-foot room with fireplaces on either end. Mount Airy Mansion was converted into a proper manor house in the 1750s and over the years played host to seven Presidents, beginning with George Washington who attended the wedding of his stepson John Park Custis to Eleanor Calvert here in 1774. The State of Maryland acquired the mansion and 982-acre grounds in 1972.

Rosaryville is primarily a picnic park although the 7.5-mile *Perimeter Trail* circumnavigates the grounds. The frequent short hills will keep your dog guessing as to what's ahead on this wooded circuit. A network of unmaintained dirt trails can also be used if you don't want to circle the park.

91
Point Lookout State Park

St. Mary's County

Take MD 5 all the way down the peninsula to the park.

Captain John Smith explored Point Lookout, a peninsula formed by the confluence of the Chesapeake Bay and the Potomac River, in 1612. The government built a lighthouse here in 1830 and William Cost Johnson bought most of the land on the peninsula in 1857 to develop as a resort. The Civil War upset those plans and a hospital for Union soldiers was built here and in 1863, after the Battle of Gettysburg, Confederate prisoners were sent to the remote spit of land.

Dogs are restricted at Point Lookout - they are not allowed beyond the causeway where the Civil War fort was located. But dogs can stay in the campground and there are loops you can share with your dog. You wouldn't want to drive all the way down to Point Lookout for it but if you are nearby there is a superb sandy dog beach north of the causeway. The Chesapeake Bay waves are frisky enough to delight any water-loving dog.

*There isn't much canine hiking but the campground
and the dog beach are good reasons to bring
your trail companion all the way down to Point Lookout.*

92
Turner's Creek Park

Kent County

The park is north of Kennedyville. Turn off MD 213 in Kennedyville onto MD 448 (Turner's Creek Road). There is no sign for either the road or the park - turn at the sign for Kent Museum. Follow to the park at the end of the road.

John Smith is believed to have met with the Tockwogh Indians here in 1608 during his voyage of exploration around Chesapeake Bay. Francis Child received the first land grant along the Sassafras River in 1671 and the surrounding land remained as family farms for the next three centuries. Private donations triggered matching fnds from the state and federal governments to create the park in 1972.

The barely discernible *Lathim Trail* - John Lathim built ships at Child's Harbour and his house circa, 1700, is now a restroom facility on the river - and *Cattail Trail* trip along Turner's Creek among massive beech and sassafras trees. There is a weathered mapboard at the parking lot that will help keep you oriented. You can use the barely-traveled Turner's Creek Road to close canine hiking loops on these out-and-back trails.

Take your dog down the small hill for superb canine swimming in the Sassafras River at the boat ramps and for extended trail time visit the Sassafras River Natural Management Area, a former cattle farm, next door.

93
Gilbert Run Park

Charles County

Eight miles east of La Plata on MD 6.

Wheatley Lake is the centerpiece of this 180-acre park. Surrounding the lake is a 2.5-mile trail, mostly swallowed by mature woodlands. Your dog will get a good workout on the hills at the back of the lake from the parking lot and long stretches of relaxed trotting as well. The St. Charles Humane Society stages its annual dog walk here.

94
Millington Wildlife Management Area

Kent County

From US 301 take MD 330 east to the park office.

Freed slaves lived on small scale farms in this area beginning in the early 1800s. The farming depleted the land and much of it was abandoned until the 1940s when the Maryland Department of Game and Fish bought 500 acres of the Toth farm for a State Game Refuge. Now Millington has grown to 3,800 acres of public hunting area.

Canine hiking here is a rustic affair on flat woodlands, consisting primarily of hardwoods. One of the primary attractions in Millington are the presence of Carolina Bays or "whale wallows." These series of shallow depressions, filled with water in rainy times, are found only in Millington Wildlife Management Area and across the line in Delaware's Blackbird State Forest. Their origins are a mystery; local lore maintains that they are the result of struggling whales, stranded after the biblical flood receded. Other theories suggest glacial scraping or even meteorites. Whatever their origins, when wet these "living museums" support rare plants and abundant wildlife.

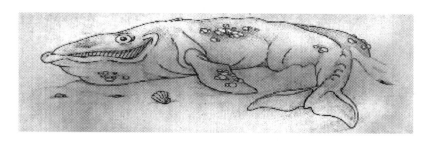

"Money will buy a pretty good dog but it won't
buy the wag of his tail."
-Josh Billings

95
Fort Washington National Park

Prince George's County
End of Fort Washington Road off MD 210; admission charged.

The first Fort Washington was completed here in 1809 and was the only defense of the nation's capital until the Civil War. Occupying high ground overlooking the Potomac River, the fort was a formidable obstacle to any enemy contemplating a water assault on Washington. When it became obsolete and a defensive installation the post was used as an infantry training facility.

Now a 341-acre recreational park, you can take your dog for a hike through the assorted military structures (not allowed in the masonry fort itself - one of the few seacoast American forts still in its original form) and on trails that lead to views of the capital and the Virginia shore, as well as down to the Potomac itself.

96
Pine Valley Nature Center

Carroll County
In the town of Manchester; from Main Street (MD 30) make a right onto York Street and turn left on Wilhem Lane after 1/2 mile to the park.

The Pine Valley Nature Center was created as an outdoor study area through a unique partnership between Manchester Elementary School and the town council. The 4.5 miles of trails here are so paw-friendly you may want to shed your shoes and join your dog hiking in the soft grass. Even the dirt trails through woodland areas are often blanketed in spruce needles.

The trail system consists of nine short paths, marked by concrete posts, that visit an appealing mix of riparian meadows and forests. Trails lead to such attractions as Turk's Spring, the Stream of Life and Avian Cove. Like the trail surface, all the climbs at Pine Valley are gentle. Stop by Walnut Pond for a quiet doggie dip.

97
Centennial Park

Howard County
On Clarksville Pike (MD 108), north of Columbia.

Within two years of opening in 1987 Centennial Park received the Merit Award for Innovative Design from the American Society of Landscape Architects. The centerpiece lake was created as a flood control measure in 1965 and now occupies 50 of the park's surrounding 325 acres.

The park features over four miles of asphalt multi-use paths, most of which are featured on the 2.4-mile *Centennial Lake Trail* around the water. This is a rolling, contoured exploration that keeps the lake in sight almost the entire way. The trail is mostly open on the south side and mostly shaded on the north where you will find the Howard County Arboreta, one of the best places to hike with your dog for an arboreal education. Many of the trees along the trail are marked for identification and most of Centennial Park's 60 or so species can be spotted from the path. This is a busy park and the lake is mostly for lookin', not swimmin'.

98
Monocacy River Natural Resources Management Area

Frederick County

Parking on MD 28 on the immediate east side of the Monocacy River bridge.

If your dog isn't partial to things like trail maintenance and maps, he's likely to love these 1,800 acres of natural areas and farmlands along the Monocacy River. The paths are unmarked and many exist only from the passing of hunters, fishermen, and the occasional horse or deer. Plan on some bushwhacking and stream crossings so this may not be the choice after a soaking rain. Also don't bring your dog during hunting season.

The main trail leading from the parking lot is an old wagon road that provided access to a quarry and lime kiln used in building the nearby Chesapeake & Ohio Canal almost 200 years ago. This is not a place for a casual 30-minute stroll; the double track road leads out for several miles with many side paths to explore, including some that lead to the river for a swim.

*Makeshift bridges are part of the adventure for your
dog when hiking at Monocacy River NRMA.*

99
Schooley Mill Park

Howard County

Southeast of Highland on Hall Shop Road between Clarksville Pike (MD 108) to the west and Skaggsville Road (MD 216) to the east.

Schooley Mill is a multi-use star in the Howard County park system. The simple trail system circles the perimieter of the 192-acre park in two concentric loops. The outer loop is a mulch-and-dirt path through woodlands and wetlands; the inner loop uses old carriage roads, often on grass. There are two miles of wooded trails and another 2.5 miles of roads through open meadows.

Much of the canine hiking is easy going as the outer trail dips into a stream valley where tulip poplars tower in the bottomlands. The trail system leads off-park in several places for longer treks. A beaver pond, packed into tight quarters, lures swimming dogs.

100
Druid Hill Park

Baltimore City

Main entrance on Madison Avenue; take Exit 7 West off I-83 onto Druid Park Drive to the entrance on the right, past the lake.

Every dog should get a romp in the big city every now and then. The City of Baltimore paid $475,000 for the Rogers family estate in 1860 to create the jewel of its park system. Colonel Nicholas Rogers designed his property to resemble a pastoral English park adthe city continued his theme with picnic pavilions, grassy promenades, statues and fountains. A massive Tuscan Doric entranceway was built of Nova Scotia sandstone in 1868 at the cost of $24,000 and Druid Lake was formed in 1871 behind the largest earthen dam in America to provide drinking water. Today the historic park covers 600 acres.

There are no formal hikes to take with your dog in Charm City's old dow-ager - just plenty of room to ramble on rolling hills. The grassy paths have long been paved over but some can still be found. The Baltimore zoo opened in Druid Hill Park in 1876 as America's third zoo and it is possible for your dog to glimpse - and certainly smell - a few unfamiliar animals as she trots about the park.

Your Dog At The Beach

It is hard to imagine many places a dog is happier than at a beach. Whether running around on the sand, jumping in the water or just lying in the sun, every dog deserves a day at the beach. But all too often dog owners stopping at a sandy stretch of beach are met with signs designed to make hearts - human and canine alike - droop: NO DOGS ON BEACH. Below are rules for taking your dog on a day trip to one an Atlantic Ocean beach on the Delmarva Peninsula.

Delaware:

Delaware State Law prohibits dogs from all swimming and sunbathing beaches from May 1 to September 30. You may also find restrictions on beaches that have been designated as shorebird nesting areas. Otherwise:

Lewes/ Cape Henlopen	From May 1 to September 30 no dogs are allowed on the beach between 8:00 am and 6:30 pm
Rehoboth Beach	Dogs are prohibited from the beach and boardwalk from April 1 to October 31
Dewey Beach	Dogs are not allowed on the beach between 9:30 am to 5:30 pm in season
Delaware Seashore	Dogs are allowed on the beach in designated areas year-round; not on swimming beaches or Rehoboth Bay at Tower Road from May 1 to September 30
Bethany Beach	No dogs on the beach or boardwalk from April 1 to October 1
Fenwick Island	No dogs permitted on the beach from May 1 to September 30

Maryland:

Assateague Island National Seashore	Dogs allowed on the beach but not on the trails
Assateague State Park	Dogs are not allowed in the park
Ocean City	Dogs are allowed on the beach and boardwalk from October 1 to April 30

Active dogs are never at a loss for something to do at the beach.

Tips For Taking Your Dog To The Beach

- The majority of dogs can swim and love it, but dogs entering the water for the first time should be tested; never throw a dog into the water. Start in shallow water and call your dog's name - or try to coax him in with a treat or toy. Always keep your dog within reach.

- Another way to introduce your dog to the water is with a dog that already swims and is friendly with your dog. Let your dog follow his friend.

- If your dog begins to doggie paddle with his front legs only, lift his hind legs and help him float. He should quickly catch on and will keep his back end up.

- Swimming is a great form of exercise, but don't let your dog overdo it. He will be using new muscles and may tire quickly.

- Be careful of strong tides that are hazardous for even the best swimmers.

- Cool ocean water is tempting to your dog. Do not allow him to drink too much sea water. Salt in the water will make him sick. Salt and other minerals found in the ocean can damage your dog's coat so regular bathing is essential.

- Check with a lifeguard for daily water conditions - dogs are easy targets for jellyfish and sea lice.

- Dogs can get sunburned, especially short-haired dogs and ones with pink skin and white hair. Limit your dog's exposure when the sun is strong and apply sunblock to his ears and nose 30 minutes before going outside.

- If your dog is out of shape, don't encourage him to run on the sand, which is strenuous exercise and a dog that is out of shape can easily pull a tendon or ligament.

Index To Parks

Printed in the United States
75753LV00005B/613-660

9 780979 557743